MAGNUS

Magnus Midtbø

Foreword

Writing a book is something that I've wanted to do for many years – to get things down on paper while everything is fresh in my memory, and as a compliment to my YouTube videos. A book all about my climbing and training, and about my travels and the people I've met. My viewers get to see a lot about my life and who I am, but not so much my story: who I really am and who I've been so far in my life – my background. That's what this book is about.

I also hope it will prove a source of inspiration and that readers will recognize bits of themselves in it, for I think that many of my viewers on YouTube have a lot in common with me. It's an experience I really enjoy, communicating and connecting with people all over the world.

This book is the real Magnus. Beyond what you see in my videos. A book gives you the opportunity to delve deeper. It's different to watching videos – the stillness of reading is a more immersive experience.

Pictures are important, too. I've picked out some of the best from many trips to different countries. Just looking at them brings back a flood of memories. When I look back now, age 33, I think about all the trips and competitions, all the people and the places, about my climbing career and about my life up to this point. It's a story that I want to share with you.

Happy reading,
Magnus Midtbø, Oslo, Norway, September 2021

Full Throttle in Preparation for China

Summer 2005 in Bergen, I drew up a plan to train harder than ever before: I would become my own slave and break down my body beyond the point exhaustion. Just keep going like a machine. Like a character in a video game, commanded to climb at the highest intensity and to only push harder the more pumped my forearms would get, fueled by the aching pain in my fingers and toes. The plan was to break myself down. Almost like an act of self-harm.

On day one, I got up at seven and ate climbing food – muesli, just like all the big guys in the sport. Then I ran down to the climbing gym with a light backpack and Green Day pounding in my ears. Part of me was dreading this day, but I was also excited, and I knew it was going to be tough. In the gym, I cranked up the volume and let heavy metal fill the dusty hall which smelt of rubber. The floor was made from car tires.

It felt good to get started, and it didn't take long before all my worries and other thoughts faded into the background. Feeling the forearms getting so pumped, like they were about to explode. Getting lowered down and immediately got started on another route. Visualizing the youth world championships in China energized me during those two intense hours in the gym.

Afterwards, I hiked up the steep hills overlooking my city and the glistening fjord, still with angry music pounding in my ears. Next up was a three-mile sprint.

My cardio was at the top of its game after several weeks in the French highlands.

After running, my body needed food: sliced bread and cereal, but not too much. I had to stay hungry. I couldn't let myself feel full. Had to keep that lightweight feeling in my stomach, ready to climb again. The afternoon would be spent in the climbing gym on yet another session, with different routes this time, more loud music and the thought of the world championship to keep me going.

This was my routine for two and a half weeks. Four hours of tough climbing and running. Plus 40 minutes of intense core exercises each night before bed, just to squeeze out whatever energy was left in my body.

The brachial artery was starting to grow bigger over my biceps as a testament to my increased strength. Even more visible were the veins on my forearms, which formed a network of light blue strings under my skin and pumped extra hard. My stomach muscles took on more definition. I began to look more like my climbing idols, with pronounced veins and visible muscles.

My body coped well with this wild ride on both the first week and the second. But on those final days, I began breaking out in cold sweats at night and it became a struggle to sleep. My body was reaching its limits. But fortunately, we were nearly at the end of the seventeen days, without wasting a minute or skipping an exercise. I didn't slack even on the very last day. Proving to myself I had the discipline to persevere, this tough training regime gave me confidence before setting off for China.

Chapter 1

Childhood

I didn't want to come out. I was already two weeks late by the time Mom lay on her bed in Haukeland Hospital in Bergen, Norway, on September 18, 1988. And I still didn't want to come out. The hours in her delivery bed ticked slowly by until almost a day had passed. A real ordeal for my mom on her first pregnancy.

Action was needed: at long last, the midwife pulled me out with a pair of forceps and she saw that one of my eyes was closed. She couldn't see any visible signs of injury, but to be on the safe side they put me in an incubator – a closed box with transparent walls for the care of premature or seriously ill babies. And so there I lay in carefully regulated conditions, even though nothing was actually wrong with me.

I recovered quickly and my closed eye soon opened. By nine months I was already walking, and in general I was an active kid right from the start. My mom had studied pedagogy but she was laid back as a parent. I had plenty of freedom to develop and explore the world through the eyes of a child.

My parents were still at college when I was born and at first, we lived in student dorms on the outskirts of town. Two rooms in a huge block, although before long we moved to a larger family apartment nearby. In 1990, my sister Hannah was born. My little brother Olav came eight years later.

My mom didn't play sports growing up, but she has always had a slim, athletic build. My dad was good at soccer and hated losing at anything, even card games. He tried out for the youth national soccer team, and he played for Start FC before his studies took over. My grandad won silver in the 3,000 meter hurdles at the national championships in 1954, became Norwegian champion in the relay and was a good skier, too.

There was natural sporting talent on both sides of my family.

Tall Trees of Paradis

People called me Magnus the Climber long before I actually took up the sport. It's a cliché that climbers begin scaling chairs and sofas as toddlers before developing a real talent in their early childhood years. They simply follow their instincts. As the philosopher and mountaineer Arne Næss once said when he was asked why he started climbing: "I never stopped".

I went to several different kindergartens. The last one was Bergen's Steiner Kindergarten out in the peaceful Paradis neighborhood of the city. A nice, almost rural spot with trees to climb. Big challenges for a small body. It felt tempting and natural to climb my way up, either with or without branches for help. Huge trees grew on the grounds of the school, with thick branches which were safe to stand on.

I climbed up to them and continued toward the top, 30 to 50 feet high, without feeling afraid. Not something that kids usually do. Especially not with a clear mind and all their thoughts intact.

One of the trees had no branches at the bottom and seemed impossible for me to climb. Straddling it with my arms or my legs was no use. One day, a guy who worked at the kindergarten lent me a pair of climbing shoes. Unfortunately, though, they were too big and I had to give up.

But I kept up on the other trees, where I felt totally at home. Nobody could reach me up on the treetops, high above everyone else with views for miles around. It felt great. I liked showing off for the girls by climbing up high, swaying in the trees and acting tough. But it was the climbing itself that drove me.

Like on square pillars. I was scaling them by the age of five and hanging from the top like a huge bug, nine to ten feet off the ground. It was enough to give any parent a heart attack, but mine held back. They could see I was in control and mom realized that I didn't take unnecessary risks. It looked dangerous, and of course it was, but I never did myself any serious harm. Even if I did fall from time to time and picked up a few scrapes and bruises.

When I think back on my childhood in the 1990s, I remember a lot of playing outdoors, lots of climbing and plenty of soccer. There were few barriers. I grew up in the second biggest city in Norway and was like a mini Tarzan – free to climb up trees and run around like a little monkey kid. This meant that I was very physically active during those golden years for motor skills, which gave me a good foundation for what came next.

A Long-Haired Steiner Student

My mom grew up in Bodø in northern Norway. Her mom had wanted to send her daughter to a Rudolf Steiner School, but there weren't any in that town in the 1970s. Two decades later, my mom was keen for me to the kind of education she missed out on. The Steiner School in Bergen was right next to the kindergarten.

There was a lot about Steiner and his so-called anthroposophical ideas that really appealed to my mom, such as biodynamic agriculture without the use of ordinary pesticides. She ate organic foods during her pregnancy with me and she was a vegetarian from the age of seventeen. She still cooked meat for us and never tried to stop us from eating it, but she disliked putting meat into her own body. I ate good food growing up. It is impossible to measure the effects of that now, but a good diet is no disadvantage.

Neither of my parents have even a tint of red in their hair. It seems my grandfather's fiery red bangs skipped a generation and reappeared in me, his eldest grandchild.

I had long hair as a boy – a strawberry blond mane that flowed down over my shoulders. A lot of people thought I was a girl, which really bugged me. My sister looked quite similar and many thought we were twins.

When we lived in the Solheimsviken neighborhood of Bergen, some of the bigger boys would threaten to beat me up as I walked home from where the bus dropped me off. One time when I was walking back, almost shaking in fear, one of the tough guys said:

"We can't beat up a girl," meaning me.

I escaped a beating that day, but I hated being mistaken for a girl.

It was mom who decided how I wore my hair when I was younger. She liked the film *The Brothers Lionheart*, based on the fantasy novel of the same name by Swedish children's author Astrid Lindgren. I said nothing and let it be until I was nine or ten years old. Funnily enough, my dad had wanted long hair growing up, but his mom insisted that he wore it short.

Cross-Country Skiing and Soccer

One Easter in the mid-90s, we went out to our cabin in the picturesque Halling Valley, swapping rainy Bergen for whiter surroundings. Skiing season was in full swing and I was keen to join in.

"Twelve miles," said my dad. If I could go that distance, I'd prove I was tough. Twelve miles on short and poorly greased skis, but I did it to prove my determination and my willpower.

I played soccer for Ny-Kronborg FC from a young age. I scored a lot of goals and ran fast, and just like all the other kids I dreamed of becoming a professional. Soccer was cool, but it wasn't my passion. I didn't watch matches on TV or learn the line-ups. My bedroom walls weren't plastered with posters of my idols or my favorite team. Soccer just didn't give me that satisfaction that you should get from sports, not even after I started playing for Brann, the big team in Bergen. And even for ten-to-twelve-year-olds, soccer involved a lot of organizing and restraints. When I started at Brann because we moved house, the coach back at Ny-Kronborg offered to pay for my bus pass.

But instead, I quit soccer at the age of thirteen. It was a good sport for learning coordination, speed, and endurance. But team sports just weren't my thing.

Magnus the Introvert

I could seem kind of strange as a kid. Sometimes friends from school would cycle a mile or two in wet Bergen weather, park up their bikes and ring the bell on our terraced house in the hilly suburbs to see if I'd like to hang out. Often, I would say no. I didn't always feel like being social.

I was an introvert. A thinker and a fantasizer. A daydreamer who let their thoughts run wild, even at school, longing away to someplace else. Unsure where, just away. Some people get like that when they have something to do. Obligations mobilize a will in me to do something else, to break free and find my own way in life, no matter what paths I've already started on. That's just the way I am.

Nattlandsfjellet, Bergen.

Chapter 2

Finding my Passion

One day in the early fall of 2000, my mom was sitting in a hair salon in Bergen when she heard one of the young hairdressers talking enthusiastically about a climbing course. It sounded exciting. I wonder if Magnus would like it? She asked me and made a call.

We went to the climbing gym at the old Bergenshallen Sports Hall and met a so-called civilian worker, Jon Egil, who was serving his military conscription at the Bergen Climbing Club. There was no one else in the hall. Jon Egil showed us what to do. He was in great shape with huge biceps and broad shoulders. A cool and funny guy who talked a lot and joked around, but a serious guy at the same time. He took big falls and it seemed like there was nothing he couldn't do.

I looked at the wall, got myself geared up, ready to try real climbing for the very first time – grabbed one of the holds and pulled myself up. I reached the top of the easiest route on my first attempt.

I wasn't especially good right away, despite having climbed so many trees and other things when growing up.

But there was something appealing about climbing in a hall that made me want to come back week after week. My enthusiasm grew. In part because I could only go once per week in the beginning so there were long gaps between each session; enough to lose interest. But the wait only made me more excited, and that made it all the more fun to go there and practice this special sport that's unlike anything else. It was magnetic in its appeal because it felt exclusive and unique. For me, it was more rewarding to be part of a small community than to pursue something ordinary like soccer.

The Draw of Climbing
The world of climbing was different and cooler than anything else. The guys who did it stood out from the more well-groomed athletes of other sports. It was a new world and a different kind of physical development, yet closely connected to my childhood obsession with climbing trees, posts and pillars.

I developed a love for the jargon and all the countless new English words I was learning like flash, onsight, free solo and crag. I learned all the unwritten rules, like never wear your climbing shoes away from the wall since they need to be really tight and uncomfortable.

At competitions, I took part in lead climbing, but I bouldered too. When I started out there was no junior category in bouldering, so I didn't really have a choice. Then came speed climbing, which I disliked because it didn't revolve around problem-solving.

Climbing was a sport on the rise in Norway around the year 2000, and I was part of a wave of young new converts. Even so, it was little known to the people of Bergen and rarely in the media. The newspapers were full of soccer players, skiers and famous faces. Climbers rarely appeared in the press and belonged to what was still a fairly unfamiliar kind, even among sports fans.

When I started out, Norway didn't have any kind of long tradition in climbing. There were no national heroes who everyone knew. The role models were mostly just known to those already on the scene. But because I didn't know too much about the sport going in, everything seemed more exciting and fresh, like my own discovery.

I told dad I had found *my* sport – a sport with everything I wanted in terms of physical challenge, excitement and community. Climbing surpassed all else and felt like something whole. More exciting than going to the theme park.

Even the way you watched competitions was different from other sports, with the audience sitting on the floor in a hall. Lots of people had long hair and wore patchy, colorful clothes. Like at a Norwegian Cup Competition at Bergenshallen a few months after my debut, when I sat and watched some of the country's best, including Jon Egil, the person I had thought was unbeatable, but who was defeated by many of the other competitors. Back then the best climbers in Norway lived in Oslo and went to the Tyrili Climbing Center downtown.

In 2001, I won a trip there to train. I stayed with my aunt Gry outside the city and took a boat in to meet some of the best guys in the Grønland neighborhood club. We trained together and it inspired me to watch them climb and hear their stories. This was my first solo visit to Oslo as a climber, at just twelve years old. A tender age when small experiences make a lasting impression. Just walking on my own around the streets of the big city made a powerful impact, and it felt great to be there to climb and to learn from others with more experience than me.

Bergenshallen Sports Hall, 2003.

One-Arm Pull-Ups

Several of the older climbers at the Bergen Climbing Club would often try to pull themselves up with one arm without quite being able to manage it. I had seen it done in videos and magazines, and it looked cool. Pulling yourself up like that in a way almost nobody else can, not even really strong guys, mostly just climbers. It's a party trick to impress others with.

I started training myself to do it by locking one arm at a 90-degree angle, first for just a few seconds, then up to ten seconds. When it comes to this kind of pull-up, most people find either the beginning or the end the hardest. For me it was the beginning. So, I locked myself into this position and practiced holding it. I spent a lot of time hanging from a beam in my bedroom and I screwed together a few planks to climb around on the wall. Not exactly safe, but it gave me my own little training den.

It helped me to hang and climb a lot. After a year of training, I finally managed a one-arm pull-up for the first time at a gathering in Bergen, and naturally it felt great. A real display of strength.

Another exercise that I couldn't wait to master was the front lever – when you hang down from a bar with your arms straight and your body horizontal in the air. After a bit of practice, I managed that one too. They were both fun techniques to master, and they took some adjusting to perfect after getting them for the first time. Physical accomplishments like that boosted my enthusiasm and confidence.

Serious Training

When I started out, it was normal to hear climbers say that they didn't train seriously. They climbed and they spent a lot of time on the wall because it was something they loved. They traveled far to nice places and waited for hours or even days for the right weather conditions. From the outside, they seemed committed to something that many outsiders considered pointless and potentially dangerous. They ate little and lived like ballet dancers when it came to food.

Climbers preferred not to admit they were serious athletes. Many outright refused to call themselves that. They weren't playing a regular sport with a coach shouting from the sidelines at practice. There was no racing against the clock, measuring your pulse or following a fine-tuned plan. They were free souls moving on the wall. This wasn't a sport but an art in motion according to some, outside the boundaries of ordinary sport. A lot of climbers wanted to compete only against themselves, or against nature, but not against others.

They climbed to be free and to express themselves in that freedom, even if many others struggled to see the freedom in hitching yourself to a rope or to bolts on a wall. Climbing was a lifestyle more than a sport.

I came to the sport after it had become established and I took it as I found it. For a kid of my generation, it seemed entirely natural to climb on an indoor wall. I started hearing people use the word gym rat to refer to people who only climbed indoors, rather than outside in real nature.

In Norwegian, people would use the term *plastic climbing*, again with negative connotations.

Sport climbing revolves around a wall which is constantly being updated with new routes, unlike the routes you find outdoors. They are literally carved in stone and remain the same for thousands of years, apart from a small degree of natural wear. I like the idea that anyone can do those routes and the metrics are always the same. That my grandkids will be able to do the same routes as me in fifty years' time. Outdoor climbing has another dimension to it compared to what you get from artificial walls indoors.

In fact, climbers do compete outdoors as well, even if not in an official capacity. There is a lot of prestige associated with different routes.

When I started at Bergen Climbing Club, it was natural for those who took their training too seriously to be taken down a peg or two. The idea was to be good without training. There was this rumor about the Christmas party. Supposedly they took tough-acting newbies out onto a bridge, stripped them naked and tossed them over, 60 feet down. So, I steered clear of that party. Rumors like that were more big talk than reality.

But even so, it was best not to stand out.

Early in my career, I accepted an offer to pose in my climbing gear for the cover of a magazine called *Norsk Klatring*, as the sport's latest rising star. It all sounded super cool. To appear on a cover like that and show my face to the rest of our extended climbing family in Norway. But some of the older climbers thought the idea was lame and inappropriate, so I turned them down.

A couple of the local papers did write about me, though. This cast a light on the sport locally and raised the profile of something which many associated mostly with a fear of heights.

In my case, I both feared and respected heights. I think all people have a fear of heights; it is something embedded deep within us given the danger involved. But no two people are the same. Some can cope with heights more easily and seek them out, without feeling paralyzed. For me, it was something I got used to, and I felt safer and more comfortable, because I started trusting the rope. But I was afraid, too, and that was part of the fascination for me; we're often drawn to things that seem dangerous.

Understanding Parents

My parents let me climb a lot even when they weren't around. They followed along and supported me, but they didn't supervise.

I liked that they kept a certain distance and that they weren't typical sports parents. This gave me the freedom and an even greater desire to do well. I wasn't one of those kids who needs or craves encouragement from home, I was happy to run my own race. It would have been less fun and less challenging if my parents had played a central role. It would have taken away a lot of the joy that lies in discovering things and figuring stuff out for yourself.

Håp for Hordalands-fotballen

ASGEIR SVARDAL
sting.svardal@bt.no

Søndag var det kretslagssamling for gutter 84. 25 spillere fra Bremnes i sør, til Radøy i nord, var samlet under kyndig ledelse av tidligere Brann-spiller Anders Giske, og Bjarne Mohn-Olsvold. Etter en treningsøkt og teori, var det klart for kamp mot Fana sitt elitejuniorlag. Kretslaget vant til slutt 7-1.

– Det nivået vi holdt i første omgang, hadde knust 3. divisjonslagene i Bergen. Jeg tror at vi holdt et brukbart andre divisjonsnivå i denne kampen, sier Mohn-Olsvold.

U-17 landslagsspiller Erik Mjelde var fremragende i sin midtbaneposisjon. Brann-spille-ren har kvaliteter som klubben kan få god bruk for i fremtiden. Pasningen til 3-0 målet var det klasse over. Fra midtbanen, vendt fra mål, vrir han seg og slår en pasning frem til Åsanes Geir Nyheim. Sistnevnte løper fra Fana-forsvaret og setter ballen sikkert i mål. Et glitrende angrep fra spillere som bare er 16 år gamle.

– Geir Nyheim er en spiller som skal score. Han ligger nok i skorpen til U-17 landslaget, sier Mohn-Olsvold.

Kvaliteten på kretslaget har bud om at fotballen i Hordaland kan få mange spennende spillertyper i årene som kommer.

sting

sting-ansvarlig Eir Stegane, 55 21 46 60. sting@bergens-tidende.no
Vanlig post: sting, Bergens Tidende, Postboks 7240, 5020 Bergen

I BULDRERROMMET: De unge klatrerne ser på mens trener Sturla Sletten gir dem et problem som skal løses. Alexander Strømme, Magnus Midtbø, Kristian Flygel (skjult), Kristoffer Bull og Christian Kjær følger med.

Med «Klatre-Magnus» mot toppen

For 12 år gamle Magnus Midtbø er klatring det gøyeste som fins. Når han var mindre var han rask opp i alle trær, men nå er det den store klatreveggen i Bergenshallen som gjelder.

HERMOD HOVE
KNUT STRAND (foto)
hermod.hove@bt.no

– Det er viktig å varme opp fingrene, forteller Magnus.

Når han klatrer er hendene det viktigste verktøyet. Dersom de er kalde kan skader lettere oppstå, skader som kan føre til at Magnus ikke kan drive med det han liker best.

– Denne veggen er ganske lett. Den klatrer jeg bare for å komme i gang, sier Magnus.

Vant i Bergenscupen

Veggen han snakker om går rett opp i 90 grader, og er 16 meter høy. Utfordrende blir det først når klatreveggen går ut over ryggen, avstanden mellom klatretakene blir lengre, og de samme klatretakene mindre og størrelse.

De ulike rutene i klatreveggen i Bergenshallen er inndelt i vanskelighetsgrader fra 1 til 10, som igjen kan ha pluss og minus etter seg.

– Da jeg deltok i Bergenscupen vinner var vanskelighetsgraden 7+, forteller Magnus.

Bergenscupen fant sted i romjulen og der ble det for første gang opprettet en egen ungdomsklasse, som Magnus gikk til topps i.

– Jeg klatrer bare fordi jeg synes det er gøy. Dessuten er det god trim, påpeker 12-åringen som klatrer fire dager i uken.

Trenger sikring

Når Magnus skal komme seg oppover trenger han hjelp fra bakkenivå. Klatrekameraten Kristoffer Bull står under og sikrer.

– Når jeg sikrer må jeg følge med hele tiden. Dersom jeg hadde stått i andre tanker og ikke holdt skikkelig fast i tauet, kunne han falt langt ned, og kanskje blitt slått inn mot klatreveggen, sier Kristoffer som ikke etter bytter slik at han får klatre og Magnus sikrer.

– Det er alltid ekkelt å falle, men når den som står under passer på, går det bra, sier Magnus.

Etter å ha vært i den store veggen en stund, går Magnus og noen av de andre opp i buldrerommet. Dette er en vegg som er litt over ti meter høy, der det ikke finnes sikring av noe slag. Dermot er det madrasser over hele gulvet, slik at det ikke gjør vondt å falle.

– Her tør man gjerne litt mer, forteller Magnus. . .

På første forsøk

Trener Sturla Sletten viser et «problem», det vil si en rute som de andre skal klare etter ham, uten å bruke andre klatretak.

Magnus er den første til å prøve ruten treneren har laget. Han klarer det på første forsøk.

– Poenget med å lage problem er at man ikke skal klare det på første forsøk, forklarer Sturla Sletten og ber Magnus prøve å lage sitt eget problem. Her får han større vanskeligheter og må ha et par forsøk før han mestrer det.

12-åringen er ikke stor av vekst, men klarer å komme seg oppover imponerende avstander. Smidig og sterk bykser han mot toppen i stor fart.

– Det hjelper ikke å ha høydeskrekk når man klatrer. Heldigvis vet jeg ikke hva det er, smiler Magnus Midtbø.

LANGT NED: Veggen som 12 år gamle Magnus Midtbø klatrer i er 16 meter høy. For Magnus er det ikke noe problem med veggen som går rett ut, den må gå utover for at det skal bli vanskelig.

STORT TALENT: I romjulen vant Magnus ungdomsklassen i Bergenscupen.

But my parents did organize vacations to go climbing in Arco in Italy, and we took road trips across Europe in the summers. Our trips sometimes lasted up to a month, with several weeks spent in Arco, filled with versatile climbing and idyllic summer living. Mom and dad learnt the basics and enough to understand what was going on, but they didn't give me advice on the sport. It was the kids in the family who knew the most, and I would explain things to dad and show him what to do.

Climbing brought us closer together as a family. We were all on different levels, but it was something fun that we could share, and which brought us out on adventures. Even if I was independent from an early age, my family has always been important. They are the bedrock of my life.

Incredible Climbing Magazines

Since climbing was still an emerging sport when I began in the fall of 2000 and because YouTube hadn't been invented yet, there were few visual sources to learn more about climbing.

I would go down to a convenience store in downtown Bergen to buy American magazines like *Climbing* and *Rock&Ice*. It was an adventure in itself to see pictures of the best in the sport scaling shiny walls or bouldering on rock. For me, these magazines were a window into an unknown world in France, Italy, Spain, the UK and elsewhere. It all seemed so distant to my hometown and to Bergenshallen. So exotically magnetic. I wanted to be and look just like the guys on the pages; just as lean and muscular, climbing my way up huge rock faces. Just like them, I wanted to visit arid, snow-free landscapes and hang bare-chested from incredible walls.

I was no bookworm and I didn't really read the papers. But my climbing magazines became regular and almost sacred reading for me, an activity I could learn from and escape into. A source of inspiration around something that I found so appealing in different ways. I disappeared into my reading and caught visions of my future self. Little red-haired me wanted to grow up to be just like the big guys in the pages of my magazines. It was as simple and as complicated as that.

Later generations who have grown up with YouTube and social media, a whole flood of information available online, might not understand how a climbing magazine could breathe life into dreams and awaken impulses in a young mind. The generation before me didn't even have the opportunity to buy foreign magazines in Norway. Books and stories told by older climbers were just about the only sources of information they had. The climbing magazines I read were like a dream world made out of words and images.

Chris Sharma became an early idol. There was something about this Californian from surfing mecca Santa Cruz, his style and the way he climbed, and his strength, too. He had his own way of doing things and always looked so cool, like a model climber with his chill, surfer-dude appearance.

I liked his explosive approach to climbing, full of energy, not always by the book, but efficient in his moves. Not always technically correct, but it worked and it was fast. I wanted to climb like that and create my own style inspired by his. He looked great in magazines and videos. He would also do this sort of roar on the wall in stressful situations, a kind of primal scream. He spoke calmly in videos and seemed like a pretty sound guy.

David Graham from Maine stood out to me as well. He was a skinny guy with nice moves who always looked cool in magazines. I hung up pictures of these two idols and of a Swiss climber in my childhood bedroom. The password to the PC on my desk was chrissharma, one word. The Americans were the coolest in part because I could understand what they said. Many of the best climbers from Central Europe spoke their own language or English with a strong accent. They didn't sound all that cool.

Bergenshallen Sports Hall, 2003. The newspaper Bergensavisen photographed me. ▶

*Hjallar wall, Sotra, outside of Bergen, 2001,
one of my first climbing photos.*

Chapter 3

An Adventure to France

In the spring of 2002, I was thirteen and hoping to join four other young climbers from the Bergen Climbing Club on an Easter trip to France. We were going to a bouldering area outside Paris, Fontainebleau, home to more than ten thousand registered boulders. I had heard and read about the forest where the French had been climbing since the end of the 1800s, and where they would go to train before taking on greater heights.

We planned to go alone without adults and without coaches – just us kids out on our own. But would my parents let me?

I asked my mom and told her we'd be with a friend who was 18. He called her and spoke to her. His voice had broken and he sounded like an adult. He was only 16, but he said he was older and promised to look after me. It wouldn't be a problem; we'd fly to Paris and get straight on the train for the final 40 to 50 miles to Fontainebleau. Nothing dangerous, nothing to be afraid of, said the voice on the other end of the line.

Mom said yes.

I packed my rucksack and all my gear two weeks in advance. I'd seen parts of the film *The Real Thing* which shows Fontainebleau and knew about some of its famous rocks and the boulder Karma 8a. Never before had I been so excited about a trip, and on top of everything there would be no parents. Just four guys and one girl.

The five of us landed at Charles de Gaulle airport in Paris and took the metro into the city, each of us with our backpack and a huge crash pad to fall onto. Definitely something we were going to need in the forest. We looked like five homeless kids lugging around our every possession.

We took the train to the little town of Fontainebleau and arrived late at night with a little way still to go. The first thing we did was swing by a store and I bought a haul of ravioli boxes, the cheapest possible food to stretch out our funds. We had heard not to leave any leftovers in the forest because they would attract a horde of snorting wild boars which would rummage about with their snouts in search of anything edible.

We stole a few shopping carts from outside the store, dumped our bags and crash pad on top and walked along the highway in the dark, past prostitutes in glittery dresses waiting to get picked up. We tried hitchhiking but nobody stopped, so we walked our way to a free campsite.

I pitched my one-man tent and the others pitched theirs and settled into their sleeping bags. Hundreds of other climbers from across Europe had made the same journey for Easter, excited to boulder in spring weather. I saw lots of cornrows and guys with long hair. It gave me a real kick to be there and just soak in the atmosphere, enjoy the vibe and to see all those tents. It seemed almost unreal to leave home in the morning and to be here by night, at this carnivalesque camping site full of fellow climbers from loads of different countries.

Before heading out, I'd heard about this French guy who got fired from a climbing store. In his anger, he went off with an axe and chopped the holds off some of the most well-known boulders in Fontainebleau. You could still see the axe marks, including on Karma. That story made an impression on me. It was fascinating to see those marks carved into the stone and to imagine that guy rampaging around with his axe.

Meeting a Hero

I spent the first day tackling a well-known boulder. In the woods that day we met a guy who looked familiar. It was David Graham himself, from the poster in my bedroom. I felt my heart begin to beat faster. This was unreal. One of my heroes standing just a few yards away – thin and hollow in his face, skinny like a jockey and with muscles sculpted by thousands of hours on the wall. He was wearing a pair of loose Prana pants. The coolest brand there was, and I knew Graham was sponsored by them. It was awesome to see somebody wearing clothes from a sponsor.

He talked with some of the guys from Bergen, but I didn't

know what to say and hung back. David set down his cell phone, his wallet and the keys to a BMW. Then he climbed the same boulder we'd been working on, in a pair of ordinary sneakers. I just watched him. What was a thirteen-year-old to say? It was enough just to watch and soak it all in.

In the evening, David Graham came to the campsite and talked to people, nestled in by the fire. I sat next to him. He was just seven years older than me, but that gap seems so huge when you're a fresh-faced teen. I was too shy to say anything to my hero that day or any of the other times we met on that trip. But it was still inspiring.

An American star sat down on the ground with a bunch of kids from Bergen one spring evening like it was nothing. Admittedly he was renting a house nearby and he drove a car, but he kicked around in the same area. We were part of the same brotherhood, doing our thing in the great outdoors, with little separating climbers at different levels. It's not like the best climbers live in mansions with huge gates all around. They don't train in closed arenas away from everyone else.

Some years later I got to know Dave and we climbed together several times. But I never told him that I was that shy kid in the background when we first met that day out in the woods.

Thor's Hammer 9a, Flatanger in the end of October 2016. It was a lot colder than it looks, only 37-38 degrees Fahrenheit.

Chapter 4

Growing Ambitions

After just a year of training, I won the National Championships in the youngest junior category in Bergen in 2001. A great achievement and one which I repeated in the years to come, but the level of competition was not that high. I wanted to compete against senior climbers in the championship and in the Norwegian Cup. But the rules said you had to be sixteen. Some felt that if a climber was good enough then they were old enough, but others didn't want to bend the rules and they had their way. But I did get to climb out of competition after the seniors and often I managed to get higher up the wall.

I did difficult routes early. The first 7b+ I did as a thirteen-year-old was called *Grønn var min barndoms salat* and is located in Loddefjord, near Bergen. In the spring 2002, I completed a route called *Øgletrynet*. An 8a by French standards, and I was the youngest person to complete it in Norway up to that point. Outdoor routes commanded more respect on the scene. Difficult ones counted more than progress on an artificial wall.

Back then, routes were set very differently in Norway compared to international competitions. The Norwegian ones were less complicated and the sport was less developed in Norway than it was elsewhere.

But the Norwegian Climbing Association gave good advice. The best Norwegian climbers, like me, suffered no hardships compared to our competitors. Even if we would often disagree in the years to come. I was headstrong and authority easily got under my skin.

In 2001, I qualified for the World Youth Championships in Imst, Austria, and I was really looking forward to taking part. But then, two weeks before the competition, we got a call on the landline at home. Dad answered while I listened from another room. I heard my name, but I couldn't make out what they were saying. I knew they were talking about me though, and I had a faint idea as to what was going on as dad looked so serious after. It was the Norwegian Climbing Association. They said I couldn't go to the World Championships because I was too young.

But the next year, with more training and experience behind me, I was able to go. I spent summer 2002 waiting to hear if I'd been selected for the youth championships in France, but word never came. It turned out the Norwegian Climbing Association thought I was too immature to participate. One day I was climbing with Lars Henriksen on Sotra outside Bergen and I mentioned this to him.

New Kid on the Block

Lars Henriksen, who also belonged to the Association, felt that I had to go and practically offered up a personal guarantee. And so, at just thirteen, I flew to Paris together with the Norwegian team at the end of September 2002, buzzing with expectations about the great and the unknown – a competition against young climbers from all over the world.

I had read and heard all about the World Championships, about Sean McColl from Vancouver who was just a year older than me and one of the best, and about blond-haired Tori Allen from the USA, who climbed with a teddy bear on her chalk bag. These two young stars shone bright in the climbing world.

We took the train from Paris to a small town and checked in to a little hotel with no restaurant. On our first night we got some food delivered to the rooms, including a salmon pizza which came undercooked. Not exactly what we had been craving. Over the next few days, I lived mostly on white bread and Nutella, which was fine by me.

It was overwhelming to look up at the French climbing wall. It wasn't like back home, it was put together in a different and more modern way, even if it would still feel out-of-date two decades later. A lot has changed in the world of climbing since then.

I'd been told we were supposed to warm up on the practice wall, but it wasn't big enough for everyone to use at the same time. I didn't want to fight for space so I held back and didn't warm up. I just watched and tried to settle my nerves. Back then, I was still afraid to fall off the wall. You could fall as far as 40 feet when lead climbing in competitions. I had a bad feeling that I was going to fall and the idea spread a negative itch through my body. But once the competition began, I forgot all about my fear and simply focused on doing the best I possibly could. I came in eleventh and top among the Norwegians.

I wasn't really confident enough to speak to foreign climbers or muscle my way into big groups. These kinds of tournaments are like youth camps and many come away with new friends. Not me though, in part because I was hesitant to speak English. Conversations felt awkward and stilted, and even though my English was actually good, speaking gave me performance anxiety. It was better to just listen and keep quiet.

The organizers invited participants to make a climbing hold, a prototype, which would be cast in a mold later on. I made my hold and took it proudly to a French judge who laughed mockingly.

"Is this a joke?" he said, suggesting that I shouldn't bother handing it in. I kept it for myself. Nonetheless, the youth championships inspired me to keep going toward something bigger and better. To become bigger and better.

Big Plans and Big Ambitions

I started dreaming about life after my career. I wanted to open a climber's hotel near Aix-en-Provence in France, where all the best climbers went to train. I wanted to run a hotel and to live, climb and spend my time someplace nice. Naturally an unrealistic dream and typical for someone my age.

I like to say that I live in the present and do things my way – I react quickly to things, put few things off and act spontaneously. It gives life a certain flow. But I also have dreams to move ahead, towards something bigger and better. To get bigger and become something more.

As a boy, I felt really small out in the world on our climbing vacations in Arco. Nobody there or anywhere else knew who I was. I was a nobody. I wanted to be known and to become somebody through climbing – to get attention and to be liked. Win praise. Those first newspaper articles gave me a real buzz. They named me Bergen's best climber; that was a great feeling. And then being crowned the best in Norway was even bigger and won me recognition from beyond my hometown.

I cared about positive attention, even though climbers weren't really supposed to. We were supposed to climb for climbing's sake. Recognition wasn't my motivation for starting to climb either, but I liked being in the papers and having others look up to me. It felt good to be recognized and to be somebody. To be good and take my space. That was a need which lay deep within me.

I didn't talk out loud about my ambitions to be one of the best climbers in the world. I might have come across as arrogant and ambitious, that typical kid with sports on the brain, unable to see that there are other things in the world

– fixated and self-absorbed. But despite this, I had a modest side as well. It felt pointless and improper to blurt out big goals. What counted was to train hard and often, to learn from the best in the sport, and get the chance to climb with them.

A Place to Train

I was given a key to Bergenshallen early on so I could come and go as I wanted. Which is to say, daily. It was nice to train alone, with such a big gym to practice in, where I could give it my all and climb my own way – quickly and efficiently. I developed my own rather aggressive style, spending as little time as possible on each route. The trick was to move up efficiently.

Was I climbing correctly?

Norwegian experts offered advice on training and technique. Others knew better than me, in part because they actually did, but also because they were more experienced. Good advice is important. But when others got involved, I would often feel a stubbornness mobilize within me. I felt determined to do things my own way, using my own physique and my own talent.

It rains a lot in Bergen and when it's raining it sucks to climb outside. Fortunately, climbers in the city had their own gym to go to. You could train all year even when it was windy and raining, all through the dark winters and during rough conditions. It was possible to climb outside at Loddefjord too because the wall overhangs.

I enjoyed climbing outside in good conditions. In Bergen, it's important to go out when the weather is nice and make the most of it. It's not right to stay inside on days like that. I understood that, but even so I spent more time indoors so that I could train more intensely and see more gains as an athlete. Your skin doesn't wear down as fast and you can get in more moves. Climbing outdoors is not as predictable.

Training Hard

I enjoyed my sessions at Bergenshallen. It wasn't packed with people like at soccer practice, but there was plenty of opportunities to advance. Full effort and full concentration. It was awesome. Up or across the wall. No leisurely movements, not one; as fast as possible, as if an opponent was coming up quickly from behind and the efforts of my upper body were to make all the difference.

Often, I would blast music in the hall and climb quickly, with my heart pounding and my forearms pumping. I loved the pump and the feeling it gave me both during and after: the way your body feels when it's been pushed to the max.

I could feel the lactic acid building up in my forearms and pushing me further. Pain and willpower were both important factors.

Some of the regulars told me not to climb so fast or hard, not to waste my energy and to use my legs more.

But I continued in the same vein. Why shouldn't I? When this kind of intense training brought progress and good results? I wanted to be the best, so it felt natural to go at things hard.

Sometimes at competitions I practically ran up the wall, forgetting to climb properly or to think about technique. I approached climbing with the intensity of a boxer, pummeling a sandbag and unleashing all their anger.

Buns and Soda

In the beginning, I would take a packet of sweet buns with me to Bergenshallen to eat when training. This was pretty normal for a kid my age; that and soda – I could easily gulp down a big bottle of coke during a day.

But advice from the Norwegian Olympic Committee in 2004 changed all that. Experts recommended regular meals comprised of wholemeal bread, muesli, vegetables, fruit, egg, milk and a proper dinner. Very much a traditional Norwegian diet, balanced and moderate. I found it easy to adapt and the change gave me noticeably more energy and less puppy fat. Good food gives you good energy. Cutting out chocolate and white sugar helped a lot.

I could see the difference in my upper body. My figure improved and my muscles got bigger. My body was still growing. At that age, boys are particularly receptive to such positive changes because your body is so vital and full of good hormones.

At the age of fourteen I measured around 5.3 feet and weighed around 130 pounds. That was pretty heavy for a climber my height.

In ninth grade, my class took a trip to the town of Järna

just outside Stockholm, the anthroposophical heart of Scandinavia with lots of buildings in typical Steiner colors and styles. I wasn't able to train on the trip and lost out on almost two weeks of climbing and other sessions, my longest break so far.

Back on the wall in Bergenshallen, my body felt totally out of shape, like I was beginning all over again. But it recovered quickly. Two decades later, I could easily go two weeks without training and still feel fit for the next session. By that stage, the strength and capacity had been built up from many years of hard training. But as a young teenager, that process hadn't really started yet.

Electronic Logs
The webpage *8a.nu* was launched in 1999 by Jens Larssen as a local climbing page in the city of Gothenburg, Sweden. It was a site where climbers could read news articles and log their routes, and it became a window out into the world enabled by the technology and new possibilities of the time.

Like many other groups, climbers started to come together online. But not everyone was pleased as a website like this easily invited competition and comparisons. Generally, most new things are met with resistance and skepticism, especially when it comes to new technology. But with time people started paying more attention, and part of the climbing world moved online where it took on its own life.

I liked logging routes and set up an *8a.nu* account in

2001. I would make a note of my routes after completing them, recording everything in detail – date, number of attempts, etc. I started blogging, too. I would make regular visits to internet cafés when away on trips in order to update my routes continuously, like a kind of climbing diary online. Updating was important to me and it gave me motivation.

There were national and international rankings on *8a.nu*. I topped the Norwegian list for about ten years and at the height of my career I was in the top three internationally. These kinds of lists meant a lot to some people, while others cared less and weren't as diligent about filling them in.

I was active on *8a.nu* from 2001 to 2015, although I stopped updating my blog a bit before. A few years later, somebody swiped my address and opened a store selling mountaineering gear in my name, without me having anything to do with it. That's the internet for you.

My Sister Hannah

After my big discovery in the fall of 2000, I started talking about climbing to my sister, Hannah, and she took it up herself about half a year later. She did athletics and was great at sprinting. It was something she had real potential in. Her physical capabilities were well suited to climbing too, even if she was a bit more muscular than most good climbers. She's also taller than many international competitors.

At first, she went climbing with her friends and I didn't exactly think it was cool to have my little sister around. We each did our own thing. When we started out, there was no dedicated youth group in the Bergen Climbing Club, but we got one soon enough.

Hannah made rapid progress too and started winning Norwegian competitions. We would climb together on our trips around Europe and soon we were heading off as part of the same team to compete. Traveling together as two siblings was fun and it felt pretty special. She wasn't as obsessed with climbing as I was and unlike me, she didn't think of it as a lifestyle, more like a sport, although one she took very seriously. She didn't drink alcohol in high school and was very focused on sports. She's a more structured person than I am, more concerned with fitting in and being like other people, not as much of a rebel. And more modest, too.

Hannah got good. She won bronze at the Bouldering European Championships in 2008 and swept the board in Norway, winning gold ten times in the National Championships between 2006 and 2017. For a ten year period we were both the best in the country, and it felt extra cool to be at the top with my sister.

Estado Critico, 9a, Siurana, Spain, December 2007.

Chapter 5

Christmas in Spain

When is a Norwegian kid old enough to spend Christmas abroad, away from their parents?

Most would say not until 18. I thought the same, and so did my two friends Sindre Sæther and Erik Paulsen when in the fall of 2003 we discussed traveling to Spain over Christmas, to the promised land we had heard and read so much about in magazines. We simply had to go, but we couldn't miss school and so that meant it would have to be over the Christmas break.

Aged fifteen, I was going to spend Christmas abroad with two friends from the club who were one and three years older. My parents let me go, just like the previous Easter when I went to France. But the south of Spain was farther away; you could practically see over to Africa from there, and I'd be away at Christmas – a sacred family holiday for many Norwegians. But I had to go and Sindre, who was three years older than me, had been the year before.

Us three teenagers boarded our plane to Málaga December 20, 2003, standing out from the other Norwegians onboard who were heading out to lounge in the sun. We had our climbing shoes and our gear, and different concerns to our flabby countrymen who just wanted to escape the chaos of Christmas.

Spain held a certain mystique for me and my friends who wanted to climb new and different walls in a warmer climate.

Before we left, we'd heard stories about this train station just south of Málaga, El Chorro, where there is just a bakery and a hostel. Apparently, this man would stand outside and shout "pan, pan" – "bread, bread", to try and attract customers. I'd heard he had stabbed his wife to death. That and other stories were all in the back of my mind as we set off for Málaga right before Christmas 2003.

When we arrived, I felt the heat outside the airport, sudden summer temperatures in December after just a few hours in the air. It felt wonderful: baking heat and sunshine, no rain and freedom from the bitingly cold temperatures you get in Bergen at this time of year. I loved the heat and found a new appreciation for it on these trips, far away from the Norwegian winter.

We took the train to El Chorro and checked in at the hostel. One bed in a room with ten to twelve others cost between four and five euros per night.

A Tunnel and a Sketchy Path
The three of us headed out to climb the next morning. There were two ways to get to the climbing area, one of which went through a dark tunnel for about 300 to 400 yards or so.

We took our chances and walked along the tracks, without getting caught by a train. Another time though, a train came hurtling towards us and we had to press ourselves back up against the wall, where we could feel the wind from the carriages as they thundered past us. There was enough clearance that our lives weren't at risk, but the stakes felt high.

The same went for the paved sidewalk outside the tunnel, El Caminito del Rey – the King's Little Path, also known as the world's most dangerous hike. It was completed in 1905 and King Alfonso XIII of Spain walked it in 1921 to inaugurate a dam. The path is barely more than a yard wide and the drop down to the river below is over 110 yards. I knew all about this unnerving trail, and I'd heard about the two people who fell down in 1999 and 2000. Back when we were there, the path was in a bad way and there were several open steps and holes in the path which made crossing extra difficult and pretty scary. Few of the original handles remained in place although there was a wire which we could hold on to. We went there with our rucksacks, coaxing our way through the worst bits. It was a lot more dangerous than climbing.

In later years the trail was closed and upgraded.

Incredible Spain

I liked Spain from the very first day. I liked the lights and the colors, which are more feminine than Norway. The mountains seemed less scary and more friendly, as if they were inviting you to come climb. Norwegian mountains have always struck me as more melancholy. I completed a route called "Swimming Through Shark Attack", an 8a+ which was as hard as any route I'd done before.

I was fascinated by the jovial atmosphere at the hostel, which was full of climbers from different countries. Like the older American climber Nick Doodle, who didn't sweat and so walked around spraying himself with a little aerosol can. Not sweating meant he didn't need to use chalk on his hands. Doodle told some funny and interesting stories, the kind you often hear from other climbers. There are always people with plenty to tell in places like this. Guys like Doodle were everywhere and they gave me a glimpse into what climbing had been like before my time.

On New Year's Eve, all the climbers celebrated back at the hostel. It was all cornrow types and a hippy-like environment, not the sort of vibe that drew me to climbing. I was there for the athleticism and the sport itself. But it was fun to watch these guys party, passing around wine bottles and other stuff. For the first time in my life, I felt peer pressure to drink, but I hadn't started with alcohol yet and I said no. I was one of the youngest at the party which had an atmosphere that grew and grew as the night went on. Somebody put an old propane burner on a bonfire, which exploded and made a noise like a bomb going off. We also had fun putting coins on the track and watching them get squashed down into flat sheets.

We would climb three days and then rest one. On one of our rest days we went into Málaga to buy groceries, missed the last train and had to walk back for three to four hours, with food in our bags and gnarling stray dogs all around. So much was different to back home.

Our Christmas trip to Spain 03/04 lasted a few weeks and felt like a kind of homecoming. I just wanted to head off again and discover new places to become an even better climber. Going to Spain over Christmas with other climbers from the club in Bergen became something of a tradition, always a highlight in the run-up to the next season and a fun adventure rolled into one.

To Shower or Not to Shower

Before that first trip to Spain in 2003, I used to shower before climbing practice. I'd come home from school, hop under the water and head off to train, freshly showered and squeaky clean. After climbing, I'd be sweaty again and need another shower in the evening. Kids are often pretty sensitive about that kind of stuff and make the effort to be extra clean. But unlike most kids, I wouldn't shower and just go to bed sweaty. Dad wondered why.

The reason was that I considered climbing to be something sacred, and that's why I washed before. And that's also why I left the smell and sweat untouched after. There was something about going to bed unshowered, taking my efforts from the wall into bed with me. Not washing away the sweat from my beloved sport. This innocent obsession lasted for about a year, until after my trip to Spain in 03/04. On that trip I realized that climbing wasn't exactly as "clean" as I had thought. Conditions were often dirty and there was no need to be freshly showered heading out. It was an obsession that makes me smile today, but something I took very seriously back then. I took everything related to climbing seriously.

Kristoffer Thorbjørnsen and I, 2006.

Chapter 6

Kiffen and Knut

From 2004 and for five to six years after, I spent a lot of time hanging out with my club buddy Kristoffer Thorbjørnsen, a skinny guy who was a year younger than me. I thought he had the perfect body for climbing as he didn't gain muscle mass even if he did a lot of strength training. That's what I wanted: to be able to train and get strong without building muscles.

Kristoffer's dad, Knut, had been very good long jumper in his younger years and he knew a lot about training. He drove us to a bunch of national competitions and to conventions abroad. He showed us some exercises and instructed us. Knut worked two weeks on the North Sea and then had four weeks at home, which meant lots of free time to spend with us.

The three of us got on well and had fun together, and success too. Kristoffer also competed at the Youth Championships in 2005. Knut put together a training program and cheered us on. Nobody was more enthusiastic, more full of that classic bounce and energy that guys from Bergen are known for. Weights, box jumping and other exercises all featured in our sessions and helped drive up our physical capacities.

"Fifty bucks", said Knut, announcing the prize money for whoever completed a route first. We liked pushing each other and trying to win the money. Others thought he was too eager and pushed too much, and that he didn't really know what he was talking about. But Kristoffer and I were happy with how things were. In Knut, we had a driver who never let us down, even on longer trips across to the east of Norway. If ever I had a coach, it was Knut Thorbjørnsen, even if he never took on the role in an official capacity. More a source of inspiration, full of good advice on how to train. The sort of guy who's always in high spirits.

Food Poisoning

Kristoffer was with us when we went to Bulgaria in August 2004 for the European Youth Cup, where we saw first-hand what life was like after the fall of communism in the East. The Norwegian team stayed at a hotel which had once been nice but was now in decline, with cats roaming the dining room. I got food poisoning at breakfast on our last day. I slept the whole flight to Munich and just about managed to drag my way over to the airport bus. The others got off but I hung back, then I collapsed twice and hit my head on one of the seats.

Medics rushed over with a stretcher. I was given some water but it spilled out and one of the nurse's thought that I'd peed myself. After being hooked up to a feeding tube and lying in a bed at the airport for a while, my body came back around. The team missed our flight and we had to take another, but luckily our insurance covered the costs after my first and only experience with food poisoning. All in all, not so bad. The worst thing that day was having my camera stolen, a shiny new one with a whole three megapixels.

Chapter 7

Raw Strength

I suppose I was born strong. Certain people are naturally stronger than others, even without training. They often weigh a ton and have huge bodies and muscles. I'm not one of those guys. I could do ten pull-ups when I was seven without training first. Hauling myself up was easy and I hardly thought about the fact that many others could barely manage a single rep.

According to Knut, the first time I lifted a barbell I was able to bench press 175 pounds. That might not sound like much, but back then I was a little squirt who weighed less than 110 pounds. 175 pounds was 60 percent more than my body weight, it was like somebody who weighs 220 pounds pressing 350 on their first attempt.

Back then I had done very little strength training, mostly just push-ups and hang-ups. I didn't do much heavy lifting in my day-to-day either, I was just naturally strong.

Even so, I wasn't crazy about the barbell or weightlifting. I didn't start chasing after personal records or trying to lift more and more pounds. It wasn't an arena that I wanted to develop in or spend time on. All my training was focused on climbing. If something didn't serve that purpose, it got dropped. Ideally, everything I did should make me a better climber. An impossible ambition in practice, but the idea behind it was serious.

Climbing so much and so intensely during those key growth years, when the body is developing and you're becoming a man, it makes you stronger. I looked strong and I was stronger than many other high-level climbers.

Ab Training

In today's internet age full of videos and images of shirtless men, there is so much focus on stomach muscles and having washboard abs. Everyone wants a six-pack they can show off, if for no other reason than to boost their self-confidence. But having a checkerboard on your stomach serves no practical purpose, besides attracting admiration and making you more attractive in the eyes of others.

In 2003, I met a Dutch guy I knew called Niels down at the Youth Cup in Europe. Niels was a few years older than me and he also spent summers in Arco with his family.

In Arco that summer, Niels had been telling me all about his abs program which he picked up at a training camp in the south of France. I should do that too, I thought, and I put together my own version: sit-ups, crunches, leg raises and other exercises. Simple movements that I could do at home without any equipment.

I started training in my bedroom in the evenings. First

eighteen reps of each, ten exercises back-to-back without a break, sweating and hurting the whole way through. It helped to build up my endurance and to strengthen my will to persevere. I went hard at in my little bedroom with rock music blasting out of the speakers on my stereo system. Maximum intensity, constantly increasing the number of reps each time – first up to 22 and then 28 in the last round. My stomach felt like it was on fire towards the end of those sessions which usually lasted around 40 minutes.

I did these exercises every night, seven days a week, after climbing in the evenings. Like some kind of bitter dessert designed to strengthen my physique and my will. They helped me build firm, bulging abs, but size was not the goal. The goal was core strength that would help me climb, and more power in my lower back for explosive bursts up the wall.

I forced myself to complete my ab workouts every night no matter what, even after competitions. Nobody else knew I did them and it made me feel like I was going above and beyond, doing more than everyone else. Like giving myself a secret edge. My family could hear heavy metal bands like Slipknot and Metallica pounding out of my room, but they likely thought I was just lying on my bed staring at the ceiling or playing air guitar.

Never Injured
It is true that I have really pushed myself and trained intensely for periods. But I don't train like that every day, all year round. Only for periods of time, like in the run-up to an

important competition. A lot like in other sports. I've always listened to my body. I slow things down when I need to, and I've had periods where I don't train at all.

Not because of injuries, though. I've never had any. I have never injured myself climbing. This makes me an outlier in a sport that puts huge strain on the fingers, arms and shoulders. A lot of climbers suffer injuries and minor conditions or ailments, but I never have. I put it down to good genes, an active upbringing and lots of training. And luck too, of course.

Different Attitudes Toward Training

When it came to training, one school of thought in Bergen went that you should climb below your limits in order to boost your anaerobic capacity. The idea was not to push hard, but stay under your pain threshold in order to gradually raise your own level. This chimed with theories from within cross-country skiing and long distance running, both endurance sports, where you switch between different intensities and zones from one to five. A mix of different intensities helped to build up capacity.

My friend and mentor, Jomar felt that these principles could not be transferred to sports climbing, which in his view was more like a combat sport. You have to go into attack mode and keep the intensity high. It can be tempting to take things at a comfortable pace, but progress only comes when you push yourself. Going full throttle is also important because we climb differently when we're tired. It's important to get comfortable being tired, to give your body the push it needs to progress. Force it to perform movements even when it's tired. Most people instinctively start to slow down when they get tired, but it's better to raise the tempo and finish faster.

I listened to the theorists, but I didn't follow all their advice. I was competing with the best in the sport and it wasn't enough for me just to do well at home. Norway was lagging behind as a climbing nation.

I had international experience and felt like nobody back home really knew anything about climbing at elite level. That wasn't true, of course, but those kinds of thoughts galvanized my anger and determination to do well at home. I didn't just want to win, I wanted to prove my total superiority over all the other Norwegians in the sport.

Jomar could see that I used plenty of anger as my driving force in climbing, almost as if I was going to battle with the wall. "Magnus had the energy of a pit bull," he said.

The Mentor Bows Out

In 2003, Jomar saw that I was becoming better than the others in Bergen. He and a few others recognized I had the potential to go far. Nobody knew exactly how far, just further than the others in our local climbing community. Jomar worked at Bergenshallen and paid close attention to everything that was going on. He was critical and it took a lot to impress him when it came to climbing.

At one point, Jomar realized that it would be a bad

idea for him to become my mentor. If I were to fulfil my potential, I would need to learn most things on my own. A fellow climber cannot guide a younger colleague to the top, especially not when the younger climber is much better. Plus, Jomar belonged to the generation of climbers who traveled around the world for years in the 1990s, with habits both good and bad that I was better off not picking up. He lived for climbing and he knew its history and folklore, and he knew many of the world's top climbers from his travels around the globe.

Jomar was interviewed a few years later when I was at the height of my career and got asked about my level. He said that if I had been a soccer player, I would have been signed by Manchester United or Barcelona. This was a comparison that most people could understand. I only earned the fraction of what a soccer player made. But still, I was earning money and getting free gear.

In 2003, I got sent clothes from Prana. This was the same brand that many of my heroes wore. Something so simple brought so much happiness and pride. A small logo on a piece of clothing meant the world to me.

In 2002, I received a grant from Bergen Municipality of around $2,500, a fortune for a fourteen-year-old. Never before in my life had I felt so rich. And I got the same grant the year after, and the year after that. Then my income doubled when the Norwegian Olympic Committee started paying me a $5,000 development grant from 2005 onward. I received support from the Norwegian state and became recognized as a top athlete. That meant a lot and it gave me status, which was pretty new for a climber. Few within the sport expected to be placed in the same category as other Norwegian athletes.

The Norwegian Climbing Association covered my expenses for trips to the World Cup and the Youth Cup around Europe. I got a fixed sum per trip. I just had to order tickets, collect my receipts and then hand them in. For domestic competitions, the Bergen Climbing Club paid half of my expenses.

Sponsorship money soon started dripping in here and there. By the time I was established internationally, I was earning good money for a climber by Norwegian standards.

I felt privileged and I remembered my dad's wise words:

"Money can't buy you happiness, but it does bring a certain freedom."

It was nice to have fewer financial concerns. But I held my spending in check and was careful to save. It's in my nature to hold something in reserve. Plus, climbing is not a lucrative sport. Nobody starts climbing because they want to strike it rich. That's why I never really liked being compared to an overpaid soccer player. They were in a whole other league, receiving enormous attention from the media at the professional level. Climbing belonged to a much more different and much smaller universe.

Chapter 8

Raging Hormones

Teenagers are bursting with hormones. Aged 16–17, a young boy is a powder keg of testosterone, bubbling all through his body. Growing up and becoming a man in just a few short years. Most kids go to school at that time, sitting down day after day, not investing those hormones into physical progress. They waste energy simply because they have so much of it. Young men also have the privilege of wasting energy because they don't know any better. They come out of childhood and become men as if by some kind of predictable surprise. Then their hormones calm down and common sense takes over.

Like everyone else, I entered into that age when the body produces lots of testosterone, but I used that energy to train and to climb. To attack the wall and find release for my sporting ambitions. While my peers got trashed and slept through half their Sundays, I was training at an elite level with manic obsession.

The separation between us was huge.

One-Track Mind

My classmates and I lived two completely different lives both in terms of mindset and physical activity. Around the age of 16 or 17, a lot of kids swap sports for parties and gigs. They live the kind of life that many young people do in the West, taking things as they come and enjoying their freedom from the responsibilities of adult life.

At that age, I dedicated my whole existence to climbing. My whole existence. I was like a kind of powerful monk, fire in my eyes, bubbling over with ambition. My mind was taken up by thoughts of routes with names and grades that only climbers understood. Why was it so rewarding to climb a route that some long-haired guy had graded 9a? Witnessed only by a small number of like-minded souls.

People outside the sport simply didn't understand it, at least not in the same way as we did. Climbers are odd. I got that, but I had such an intense relationship with climbing that my mind didn't care about anything else.

As a teenager, I didn't really hang out with my peers from school. I preferred to spend time with the guys from climbing, both older teens and adults. I felt a sense of belonging in their company. It was a world of travel and adventure, completely different to what most Norwegian teenagers cared about.

For many years my life was dedicated to climbing and only climbing. From getting up in the morning to going to bed at night, everything revolved around climbing. My mind was constantly fixated on routes, trips, training and gear. Nothing else was able to capture my imagination. I'd practically get offended if a classmate asked me to go to the movies.

The movies? Why would I waste my time sitting in a dark room watching a screen? It seemed idiotic. How would that help my climbing?

The same went for alcohol and partying. I completely avoided all that in Bergen. I didn't socialize with my classmates outside of school, not even at high school graduation which is a huge deal in Norway. I missed out on a lot of fun and typical teenage experiences, no doubt, but it just simply wasn't possible for me to give my all to the sport and to have a normal adolescence at the same time. It didn't feel like a sacrifice to keep away from drinking, partying and all other excesses. In fact, it was actually doing that stuff that felt like the sacrifice. It meant sacrificing progress in my climbing. And that just wasn't on the cards.

People told me I could never become the best in the world. Not a kid from Norway, we didn't have the traditions or the renown within climbing. That was reserved for other nationalities. The French, the Italians, the Americans, the Austrians – to name a few. Those countries had bigger environments for climbing, places I visited to become better.

In The Grip of Pain
I have a really high tolerance for pain. It's something all climbers need, with lactic acid pumping out of your forearms until they feel almost dead from the pain. You can't go far in

climbing without a high pain threshold.

The ability to withstand pain is both something innate and learned. You push the limit and let your body take a beating on multiple fronts while climbing, for as long as it lasts – a few minutes, an hour, two hours. Climbing means pain in your fingers and skin peeling off. Numb fingertips that regain feeling on the wall.

I liked all of that.

But I still wanted to be comfortable and sleep well, and not subject myself to endless torment of the sort some climbers seek out on their expeditions. I didn't want to ache and hurt for days on end while away. Too little food or sleep meant feeling cold for hours on end. I didn't want to climb like that. Longer expeditions and overnighting on the wall have never appealed to me.

Skipping School
As a kid, I never played hooky from elementary school. I missed more class in middle school because of climbing but with valid reason, and often an email to the school from the Secretary General of the Norwegian Climbing Association. I usually went off with the others from the Norwegian team to compete on Fridays. This continued for years and even through high school.

It was an adventure to fly off on Thursday nights or Friday mornings and go somewhere in Europe, like Arco in Italy. Away from Bergen where it was windy and rainy, escaping everyday life for what I truly loved. Climbing with my buddies and acquaintances from many different countries. It was like going off to a dreamland for a couple of days and then flying home again, back to my Steiner School and its hateful choral singing and eurythmic dance. Like a punishment for having such a good time at the weekend. As if life simply couldn't be that good all the time.

I started to miss even more classes in high school. Once I first crossed that threshold and skipped school without explaining why either before or after, without permission or good reason, my absenteeism went up to more than half.

Tricking mom to get off school was easier than tricking dad. So, I'd just stay in bed until dad had gone to work and then ask mom if I could stay home because I wasn't feeling well. She said yes more times than not, especially after my parents divorced in 2005. I was glad when they divorced. They'd been fighting a lot.

I continued living with mom and realized it was easier to get my way without dad around. Much of what I wanted revolved around climbing. She said yes because she considered it to be a healthy interest that gave no cause for concern. She wasn't worried about me falling or getting hurt because I told her it was safe and that I used a rope. Of course, there was a lot she didn't see. She lived in blissful ignorance about a lot that went on.

In the fall of 2005, I considered dropping out of high school and moving abroad to commit myself full-time to climbing. School was a nightmare and my absences were racking up. I felt like I had nothing to do there, little in common with the other students, and so there was no point sitting at my desk and staring at the board, listening to teachers drone on and on.

Because Steiner students set the curriculum themselves, I couldn't take textbooks and stuff away with me on trips like other students could. This meant that I missed out on even more of my education and everything else that was going on. I had to check in with the others from my class and ask for updates on what I'd missed.

Céüse, 2005.

*The Forbidden City, Beijing, China, 2005.
From the left: Kristoffer Thorbjørnsen, I,
Hannah and Malin Folkestad.*

Chapter 9

Among the Best in the World

I started competing in the European Youth Cup in 2003. Tough competitions across the continent against the best in the sport.

I won the European Youth Cup in Kranj, Slovenia on November 27, 2004. My victory came with a huge trophy which we took with us on our trip out of the country by minibus. Me and my Dutch friend Niels – the one who had shown me his abs program – travelled along with the Austrians back to their country.

"We've got to go there," Niels said, "we could both learn something." The weekend after the Youth Cup was the World Cup for seniors in Kranj and we were both going to take part. Rather than go home, we decided to travel to Innsbruck in the west of Austria for a few days instead.

It felt exciting to be riding back with the Austrians, who I didn't know very well at that point. We both thought the whole experience was really cool. I felt very international. Part of something that stretched over borders. Traveling unsupervised at the age of sixteen.

The bus dropped people off at several different places around Innsbruck, which was home to many of the climbers. Niels and I got off outside a real classy hotel and strolled in with our bags, looking out of place with our big rucksacks in that elegant reception.

"You two can't afford to stay here," said the man behind the desk, looking at our clothes and age, taking us for a couple of misguided interrailers.

His attitude provoked Niels, but I just took it in stride.

Katharina Saurwein was one of the Austrian climbers who lived in the city, still with her parents, and she invited us to spend the night at hers. Her boyfriend, Jorg Verhoeven, lived there too and was somebody I admired. He wasn't there that night, but even so it felt pretty cool to sleep over in the same house that he lived in.

The next day, Niels and I went to the Sport Hotel in Innsbruck, which is right by the climbing center and intended for visiting athletes. We were met with a warm welcome and cheap rates. I would stay there a lot in later years. You have to belong to a national team to stay, so the Norwegian Climbing Association booked my room.

Over the course of that week in late November of 2004, I saw how the best Austrian climbers trained. They did a lot of stuff like I did. It was reassuring to see. I also saw kids as young as seven or eight climbing at a really high level. Climbing was a popular sport in this country.

After a couple of days, Niels and I took a long and tortuous journey on the train to Kranj. We showed up like a couple of fresh-faced punks and went up against some of the best seniors in the sport. I was one of the youngest in the competition and came in around 50th place. Nothing to brag about back home, but fun and insightful. I was already looking forward to next season. With each year that went by, I got to experience more and meet more people, visit new places and do more climbing.

A Summer of Hope

The summer of 2005 was an eventful one in my life. At the end of May, I came in 15th at the World Cup for seniors in Imst, Austria. Then I finished 27th out of 130 at the World Championships in Munich, and still at just sixteen years old, again one of the youngest in the competition.

I went to Céüse in France to climb and felt on top of my game. That Summer I did a route called Le Cadre, an 8c by France standards.

One day I forgot to eat breakfast and began climbing on an empty stomach, which was out of character for me. Things went surprisingly well. My body felt nice and light. It was enough simply to drink before the session. That realization stayed with me, something to be explored later on.

Everything seemed fun and life just flowed along. One day at a country estate in the south of France, I happened to meet Jack Osbourne, son of Ozzy Osbourne, who were both huge at the time because of their reality TV show. It was a bizarre experience to play table tennis with him and to be around his sister Kelly. Both were there to get into shape and lose some weight, and their diet featured as part of the show. It was hard to believe that a little kid from Bergen like me was standing across a table tennis table from a global TV personality. Climbing sure can take you a lot of unexpected places.

I was full of pep. The big goal of the season, the World Youth Championships in China at the end of August 2005, was at the forefront of my mind. All on my own and without consulting with anyone, I drew up a training plan in preparation for my journey there. It was a detailed plan for me to follow in Bergen over those two and a half weeks I had available. Nobody else knew about my plan when I came home back to an empty house in the hilly suburbs of Bergen. Mom was on vacation and dad was living someplace else. They had just divorced.

And so began the intense period of training that opens this book. Many grueling hours of climbing and exercise each day, sometimes with Kristoffer Thorbjørnsen and his dad Knut. They were very involved and provided a lot of inspiration.

It was around this time I discovered coffee. Drinking some helped me get going in the mornings. Undergoing a late puberty helped too. I really felt like a boy turning into a man, like I was getting stronger and more powerful by the week. It's an awesome feeling and I felt immortal. The goal now was to improve upon my fourth place from the World Youth Championships in Edinburgh the year before. I wasn't aiming to win in China, I just wanted to do better.

World Youth Championships in China

Asia is a long way from Norway and this was to be my first trip out of Europe, my first experience flying long haul and my first time getting jetlag. Not to mention sitting still on a huge plane for eleven hours. My sister Hannah was also there as part of the Norwegian team, and so were Kristoffer, Malin Folkestad and our group leader Siri Dragset from the Norwegian Climbing Association.

I was exhausted after training so hard and I just wanted to sleep when we arrived at our tiny hotel in Beijing. Going off to see the Great Wall of China just wasn't on the cards, my body needed only two things – rest and food. The only thing edible at breakfast was the whitest bread I'd ever seen, unfamiliar to a guy like me who mostly eats wholemeal. We had to order at the table from local servers, who just watched on in disbelief as I asked for more and more, wolfing down about 30 slices of bread.

I had bought a stick of Toblerone at the airport on arrival, and it went down a treat that night as well. My body simply absorbed whatever I gave it after two weeks of torment. Unsurprisingly, my stomach did not react well to all that white bread and Chinese food, unfamiliar to a Scandinavian guy like me, with different bacteria in my gut to what the Chinese have.

Competitions in Asia and other far-flung places required extra caution: you had to be careful about what you ate to avoid food poisoning. Unfamiliar food doesn't always sit right in the body, especially in combination with the change of time zones. In China, the team soon decided to eat dinners at Pizza Hut, which served up familiar dishes like those we ate back home. Pizza there was expensive and a waiter opened the door to us each time we went there.

I started the competition on August 25 feeling sluggish. But things loosened up on the second round. My body started doing exactly what I wanted it to and then some. I felt a kind of raw strength, superior to the others, and I won. At previous competitions the margin was often just a single hold, a single point. This time the margin was ten. I won and got higher up the wall than anyone else in both the semi-final and the final, outperforming even the oldest in junior class.

It felt great to stand on the podium and hear the Norwegian National Anthem being played in China, while my sister Hannah, Kristoffer and the other Norwegians all sang along. It just so happened I was wearing normal clothes at the time, not national colors and no Norwegian flag on my chest or back. One of the parents came over and praised me for it: I represented humanity, not a particular nation.

The title world champion has a special ring to it. It means something special within the world of sports. I could really feel its glow at the banquet after, all those pats on the back and strangers who wanted to chat with me. It was cool to hang out with four hundred other young climbers from all over the world and to make so many new friends and acquaintances. Austrian climber David Lama was there and won in the youngest category. We met properly for the first time and immediately clicked, even if he held back a little and didn't speak with everyone.

*China, 2005, ready to climb the
finals, I was excited and felt strong.*

After the award ceremony at the
Youth World Championships, 2005.

First Love

At the World Championships I met Miranda Guzzo from Canada. She was one year younger than me. Sweet, charming and easy to talk to. We ventured out one evening into the chaos of the city, surrounded by traffic. Two naïve, young teens in a faraway land. We talked like kids that age do and walked together to be on our own, away from the others.

She was popular with other climbers too. David Lama joked that she only spoke to me first because she couldn't work up the courage to speak to him.

On the flight back from Beijing I thought only of her, Miranda, and when I might see her again. Both David and I thought about her a lot for a while. I sent her emails and kept in touch for a bit, and I longed for her but told no one. I kept that sort of stuff to myself and saw no need to talk about it. In a way this made me a little more secretive and reserved. Nobody needed to know anything.

Nothing more happened with Miranda. We lived far away from each other and we were young and totally inexperienced when it came to dating. Before her, I'd only ever had small crushes at school. And even though nothing serious ever happened between me and Miranda, she was still my first real love interest. Just having these kinds of feelings was a new discovery for an introverted climbing kid like me. Suddenly a girl was on my mind, and it surprised me how much. It felt nice and unfamiliar in a good way. I had something new to occupy my thoughts with besides just climbing, even if she did belong to that world as well.

The best of class Youth A, China, August 2005.
From the left: Felix Neumärker, Germany, I and
Sachi Amma, Japan. I used my casual shirt,
without the national colors, and with a Canadian
pin on my shirt, that Miranda gave me.

Chapter 10

David Lama

In December 2005, I flew to Barcelona by myself, buzzing with expectation, and waited eight hours at the airport. Then David Lama arrived from Austria together with his mother. She had agreed to drive as neither of us had our license yet.

She hired a car and we drove down to Siurana, a village with a Medieval castle and fewer than fifty permanent residents, and one of the most famous climbing areas in the world. We shared a room in a small boarding house. David's mom had a room to herself. It was cheap and cheerful with everything we needed, including food. Plus a few other climbers who were also down over Christmas vacation.

On the first day I flashed an 8b+ and onsighted an 8a+. David led away and was hungry to try more and more. We pushed each other forward. There was no question of stopping while there was still daylight. Success just made us want to keep going, preferably onto something more difficult.

David spoke low and soft, in a restrained manner without much fanfare. But still with an energy that encouraged other climbers to push on and continue, to do more the same day or the next, wherever he and I had been climbing.

For David, nothing seemed impossible. He saw no limitations as a climber and he had plenty of confidence in general. It helps to believe in your own abilities. And he had good reason to, his movements were light and fast like a cat. His climbing looked effortless as he glided along in his own distinct style. He had begun climbing in a proper gym when he was just five-years-old and got in a lot of movement from an early age.

During that Christmas trip in Spain, David insisted that we both sat in the back of the car to talk while his mother drove. It felt like we had our own private chauffeur as we zipped around from place to place. His mom went above and beyond to help out her only child. It was strange for me to have somebody there who took care of everything. I was used to sorting most stuff out for myself. For David, this was normal and naturally he was happy.

After a few days, we drove across to Santa Linya. It was a relatively new climbing spot and there were no official guidebook from there. But luckily, we ran into Spanish climber Dani Andrada at a café and he drew up the lines on a napkin for us. It was cool to be handed a napkin like that from such a good climber.

Not only that, he was there with Chris Sharma himself – chill and content. My pulse started racing when I saw this hero of mine, who seemed super friendly and spoke with an American accent. He was so cool but I couldn't bring myself

Those intense days in Spain that Christmas left me more worn out than any other climbing trip. I started falling on easier routes over the last few days and I could feel that my body needed to rest. We agreed that I would go to Innsbruck that summer and stay with him. And then we went home, each of us inspired by the other.

The route Non stop. David had to use my jacket around his waist to keep warm. I kept warm by having hot stones in my chalk bag. ▶

*Terradets, Spain, Christmas 2005,
David Lama to the left. He helped
me out on the route Non Stop, 8b. I
was able to Onsight it.*

Chapter 11

Too Heavy

By winter 2006, I was starting to feel that I weighed too much and wanted to lose some muscle mass. A junior world champion with ambitions to win the World Championships as a senior couldn't weigh "a whole" 140 pounds. Still, I was lean. Skinny according to some. There was little fat to trim away, but I had muscle to lose. My sister had recently lost weight and her performance got better afterwards. She was a vegetarian, so I decided to cut out meat to slim down.

I started eating less and only at regular times. I didn't talk to anybody about dieting and did most of my eating on social occasions, so others got the impression I was eating more.

Soon I could see my muscles more clearly in the mirror. Veins lay over my arms like long, snaking strings and my abs looked like pork chops. Everything looks more defined on a body with less fat. There's also something about decreasing your fat percentage that feels natural for a boy or a man. It puts you more in tune with yourself and brings relatively more muscle mass.

I associated feeling hungry with something positive. It

made my body seem lighter and more muscular. My muscles were more visible on my stomach and everything felt tight in a good way. Plus, everything tasted better the less I ate, even food that I used to chuck into me without much appreciation. An apple and a handful of grapes suddenly tasted incredible. A slice of bread was like a delicacy.

I looked forward to mealtimes and I ate the same thing each day: three apples a day, two slices of wholemeal bread and two hard-boiled eggs for dinner, plus a salad with a little olive oil drizzled over. Or almonds or hazelnuts chopped up and sprinkled on top. I would count out each individual nut and have the same number each day. The anticipation before a particular meal was something I enjoyed, and it felt nice to know exactly what lay ahead.

I stopped eating breakfast. I wouldn't eat anything at school, I'd just take a 50 oz bottle of water with me and drink it fairly quickly over the course of the day. Preferably without anyone noticing. The others would only wonder why I was drinking so much, so fast. I constantly had to go to the bathroom and it felt like such an effort with so few calories in my body. It was best to just stay in the classroom with my down jacket wrapped around me to keep warm. It's harder to keep the heat in on a heavy calorie deficit, especially one that stretches over several months and at an age when your body needs a lot of calories. Other kids my age ate a lot because they were growing so much. Arts and crafts, a class I liked, took too much energy out of me because I had to stand up and do something physical. When things felt heavy, climbing

Qualifications for the Norwegian cup,
Vulkan climbing center, Oslo, 2006.
My body weight was only 127 lb.

Turning Point

Weight loss was like a dark cloud over our family in the winter and spring of 2006. Others could see that both my sister and I had lost a lot of weight. She had an eating disorder as well and was climbing at a very high level. Mom realized that things were serious and rang up the coach of the national team to vent out all her worries. Something had to be done.

I remember one day down in the laundry room in the basement, beside the dryer around May 2006. I was standing there in just my pants, with my bones and ribs sticking out. Mom realized then just how thin I was. She started crying and went into a state of despair. She didn't want to believe that she had two kids who hardly ate and had lost so much weight over the winter. I could see and hear how distraught she was and I realized that things had to change. I couldn't go on living like a prisoner of war. It was time to start eating properly again.

My body absorbed nutrients like a sponge and I gained weight quickly after so many months of hunger and undereating. My muscles grew and my energy levels recovered. A lot happened to my body in just a few short weeks. The changes were so visible that some adult climbers mumbled about me taking anabolic steroids to quickly grow muscles. That of course was not the case.

My natural predisposition for muscle growth and being at an age when the body produces a lot of testosterone meant that conditions were ripe for building muscle mass. The same discipline that led me to lose so much weight helped me back to a more normal diet. My body was out of balance and looked strange, almost disjointed. It took practically a year before I felt totally myself again.

Even afterwards I was still careful about my weight and conscious of my diet, and I continued that way. Most elite climbers are conscious of their weight. It's important to feel light and nimble. I loved that feeling of weightlessness. Climbing and feeling so light you can pull yourself up without effort, in a single movement, as efficiently as possible.

Fully grown, I could cope with a weight of 138 pounds. Any less than that and my body would feel weak in a way that would affect my climbing. I'd feel stronger at 143 pounds, but my endurance was better at 138. It was all a careful balancing act between lightness, strength and endurance. I even competed at 149 pounds. But if my body had been able to withstand and function at 120 pounds, then that's what I would have aimed for. That's how desperate I was to rise and to have the optimal body for the sport.

Siurana, Spain, the crux on Jungle Speed, 8c+, 2015. It was originally graded 9a, but I put it as 8c+.

Bern, Switzerland, 2009, Mammut had the photo shoot, 160 feet above the ground.

Chapter 12

Summer in Austria

By the time I went down to David Lama's in the summer of 2006, my weight was on its way back up and I felt strong again. But even so, I was still out of balance and not yet fully recovered from my intense dieting. I slept in his childhood bedroom, on a mattress on the floor. His chubby house cat would lie next to me, and one morning I woke up and couldn't open my eyes. They were stuck together and it felt super uncomfortable. It looked almost comical.

David's mother was worried about me and thought that perhaps I needed more meat in my diet. They poured water over my eyes and slowly they opened again, but it took a while before we realized the cause: I was allergic to cats. Keeping the cat away solved the problem.

I was still a vegetarian even as I found myself in a house with plenty of meat on the menu. David's mom asked if there was anything in particular I'd like her to make. "Nah," I was happy to just eat potatoes and vegetables at mealtimes. That was fine for me, though I felt like a real outsider at a barbecue in the neighborhood because I neither ate meat nor spoke German.

David was still only 15-years-old, he was a cheerful guy and a global climbing talent. He climbed in the final without tying his shoe laces just to show off how much better he was, and he won all the same. He made little jabs at the most serious guys in the sport who thought only about training and getting better, the guys who didn't even let themselves cut loose a little bit afterwards. I did something quite similar in Norway to mark my superiority.

David didn't take himself too seriously and he made fun of climbers who only thought about training. I got where he was coming from. Like the Swedes, for example, who lived like monks but didn't really get to be all that good. I couldn't help but snigger at them. I didn't want to be like that. Once at a competition someplace I saw them jogging and using resistance bands to warm up. I just cast myself full pelt at the wall without warming up and I beat the Swedes all the same.

At home in Innsbruck, David loved hanging out at his local climbing gym and talking with people, not just climbing. Just chilling in that environment. But by the summer of 2006, he wanted to spend more time out on bigger walls and I tagged along. We spent less time training in the gym, what I called proper training, focused on competitions. During that period, it didn't seem like David was much into strength training or working towards goals in sport climbing. He mostly just wanted to climb outdoors.

A Good Place to Be

A lot of great climbers live in Innsbruck. Dutch climber Jorg Verhoeven hung out with David a lot and he had his own car by summer 2006, so the three of us drove across to Chamonix, France, for the World Cup there. Jorg is a well-read guy. Musical and philosophical, a bohemian type. He's also really social and well-liked. He was one of those guys I had looked up to and admired, read and heard about, and then become friends with. A lot of my friendships started that way because we'd meet at competitions and other places. It felt cool to train with somebody I had looked up to.

Jakob Schubert lived in Innsbruck as well. He was two years younger than me and we looked quite similar. We both had red hair, although he was an inch or two taller and a little skinnier, with more defined muscles. A real athlete. At the Tivoli Climbing Center in Innsbruck somebody came up to him once and said:

"I saw your brother here earlier," meaning me.

A lot of people thought we were brothers. The funny thing was that Jakob also had a sister who was a year and a half younger and she was also a climber called Hannah. Jakob had been training a lot for many years, starting off very small and slender, with scrawny arms. He went on to become one of the most athletic guys in the sport.

In 2006, David got me onto the team at Mammut, a Swiss climbing brand which sponsored climbers. For the first time in my life, I was getting paid by a sponsor, a few thousand Swiss francs per year. It felt great to be on the same team as

David who was earning even more. Different climbers got paid different sums.

In the summer of 2006, I spent a couple of months in Innsbruck with David and Jorg. A wonderful and carefree time when we were young and free to climb and explore. David had a playful relationship to the sport. But still an ambitious relationship. Even back then he dreamed of scaling huge peaks and completing difficult routes out in real mountains.

He had the mental stamina for challenges like that and had no problem enduring pain over long periods of time, even days. He could survive on little sleep and food, put up with freezing cold temperatures and discomfort, all without losing his spark. After David started going on expeditions, he often had a limp or some other problem, like after he fell forty feet into a stream and knocked his coccyx in less than two feet of water. He was black and blue afterwards. But it didn't faze him. It was all part of being a climber.

As an experienced adult mountaineer, David said:

"What we do in the mountains surely has nothing to do with Russian roulette. It's more like poker. It's really something you think about. You weigh out your chances. You only take the risk at the right moment … On the mountain, you must really overcome your weaker self. But in the end, you get paid back."

One day in the fall of 2007, he, Jorg and I were climbing outside Innsbruck and got ourselves about 330 feet up a wall. A woman appeared down on the ground and started shouting up at us. We waived back at her without thinking twice. She mistakenly thought we were in trouble and rang mountain rescue, who quickly arrived in a helicopter while we were still high up the wall and doing just fine. We realized the misunderstanding and kept climbing in the hope that the helicopter would realize too and fly off again.

In the end we rappelled down, a little worried that we'd have to pay a fine for wasting public resources. The pilot and the others stood and waited. We didn't have to pay anything because the misunderstanding wasn't our fault. David continued competition climbing for another three years and then quit in 2009.

A secret project I was allowed to try in 2016, outside of Stavanger. It is a project and the grade is not set yet.

Stranded in England

In April 2010, David Lama and I went on a team trip for Mammut to the Peak District in England, to a well-known climbing area close to Sheffield.

When we got to the airport in Birmingham to go home, all flights were grounded due to the Icelandic volcano eruption, which was spewing out lava and black ash clouds that paralyzed air traffic all across Europe. The event gave rise to a new word in Norwegian: "askefast", which literally means "ash-stranded". It was a word used to describe people who were stuck abroad because of the ash cloud.

David and I ended up "askefast" at the airport, waiting around for hours and hours with very few other passengers around. We weren't sure whether we would get home at all that day and we started goofing around to pass the time.

Just for fun, we pretended we were two completely different people: David was one of the world's best tennis players and I was his manager. We told this story to the other passengers we met, who perked up their ears when they came across us talking convincingly about the tennis high-life we were claiming to live. Just two kids goofing off to kill time while we waited.

But we soon realized that no planes were taking off and hired a car to drive back to the Peak District for more climbing instead. We got to spend a couple of really great bonus days there while air traffic was at a complete standstill over much of Europe.

Peak District, England, after the Icelandic volcano eruption in 2010. An English E5.

The Last Trip

From 2010 onward, David went off on a lot of expeditions and made a life for himself as a professional mountaineer. We had little contact for a number of years, but I followed his adventures. He seemed almost immortal, able to survive whatever came his way in climbing.

In April 2019, he climbed Howse Peak in Canada together with fellow mountaineers Jess Roskelley and Hansjörg Auer. They reached the top on April 16, 2019 and got caught by an avalanche on their way back down. A shiver ran down my spine when I heard. I turned on the news and brought up articles online. I still believed that David could survive anything and I hoped they would be found alive. I sent a message to Jorg Verhoeven and got a worried response.

All three died in the avalanche and were found five days later. David Lama was 28-years-old.

David Lama to the left and I,
Peak District, April 2010.

I waited for the ferry in Denmark, in the fall of 2011, on my way home after the best season of my career. I slept in the car and felt free.

Chapter 13

On Wheels

I got my driver's license in the fall of 2006, aged 18. That awesome little card is like a trampoline out into the world and brings so much freedom – just as long as you have a car. I got an old Honda Civic, but it was almost ready for the scrap heap and I wasn't willing to drive it to Spain for fear that the engine might give out.

In February 2008, I went to Spain to climb in Santa Linya together with Tor Willy Ingebrigtsen, whose girlfriend was studying down in Barcelona. He and I climbed together at first, then he went off and I was left all on my own, in a cave where I had come to try a 9a+ route – *La Novena Enmienda*. Nobody as young as me had managed such a grade before.

I slept in the cave in a summer sleeping bag, unsuitable for winter, and shivered my way through the night. I liked being alone and outdoors 24 hours a day. The rising sun felt good in the morning, so I would sit and warm myself up in the sunshine. No gas stove meant a lot of bread and rice cakes for sustenance, a diet of mostly dry and simple foods. A flickering bonfire provided warmth and a pleasant atmosphere in the evenings.

One day, a car came driving along carrying two parents and their son, Adam Ondra, already a recognized wunderkind in the world of climbing. This 15-year-old kid made quick progress and completed the 9a+ route that I'd been working on. Adam flexed his skills and moved quickly on to new challenges. He was the youngest in the world to do such a difficult route.

A little later, an American entourage parked up near the cave in a little rental car and offered me a spot to spend the night in their already over-crowded car. An irresistible offer to get out of the cold. I slept sitting upright in the seat, so my sleep quality still wasn't exactly optimal.

I completed the 9a+ route in February 2008 and I was delighted. I was the second person in the world at that level to do it, after Adam Ondra. The Americans took off in their car and I was left alone in the cave again for another week.

Time to Move?

Constant trips all over Europe were one of the reasons I missed so much school those last few years in 2006/07. I didn't complete school or get my high school diploma. I moved to Oslo in 2007 and I've lived there ever since. My mom and sister lived there as well while my dad remained in Bergen.

I had planned to move to Innsbruck in December 2007 after a Christmas trip to Spain. The idea was that I'd fly to Munich and buy a car then drive to Spain with Kristoffer right before Christmas. After a few weeks of climbing, I'd go to Innsbruck in the New Year and look for a place to live. All the best climbers lived there or nearby and it offered perfect conditions for climbing, inside in winter and outside in summer. Plus, it was just a couple of hours by car from Arco. So even if it was snowy and white north of the Brenner Pass, summer was just two hours away. I dreamed of living and training in that part of the world, with my own car for the first time, completely independent.

But in Munich, the car salesman refused to sell me anything without a permanent address either there or in Austria. So, I had no choice but to rent a car for the drive down to Spain, and the move to Innsbruck never happened.

A Home on Wheels
In the summer of 2009, I bought a Ford Transit Connect and put a bed in the back to create my own little mobile den. I felt like a king on four wheels back there and had everything I could possibly need. Plus, it cost hardly anything to run and meant zero rent to pay. A dream come true – I had always wanted to just drive around from place to place, climbing and hanging out with friends, just like so many others before me. It meant forming part of a long tradition within climbing. I would spend the period between April and November on the road, exploring new climbing spots and meeting up with fellow climbers to train and compete together.

I never felt more free than when driving my car across Europe, with no fixed destination and the freedom to sleep in my car. I could stop whenever and wherever I wanted, sleep and then move on. This was how we had spent our family vacations when I was growing up; we took the ferry from Oslo or Kristiansand, either to Germany or Denmark, and we drove on from there. Climbing allowed me to travel about in much the same way as I did when I was younger. It was an opportunity to continue with that lifestyle as an adult and even to visit places like the USA.

I made it a challenge to do the drive from Norway to Spain without stopping to eat. Just water and coffee, a few hours of sleep and then back on the road. Traveling like that suited me well. It kept me focused behind the wheel, got me excited about climbing and it meant my body would feel lighter on the wall because it physically would be. I'd lose about three and a bit pounds on those two-to-three day trips – no doubt mostly water weight, and pretty noticeable on an already lean body. This was my way of preparing to climb and a kind of internal competition between me and myself. It wasn't something I spoke out loud, just something I did.

Having normalized my weight after the diet in 2006, I still liked the sensation of being hungry. I found that it improved my performance just so long as I also got enough nutrition. Being in that state makes you more primitive, like a predator searching for prey out of hunger, out of necessity. It's not something I thought too much about, but that's how I felt at the time.

Holmenkollen ski jump tower, Oslo, 2015, photo shoot with sponsor Norrøna. The tower is 200 feet above the ground.

Research has shown that the body begins to produce more testosterone and growth hormones once it has gone about sixteen hours without food. The level kicks up a notch and nature gives us extra energy to find sustenance. But I had no idea about intermittent fasting back then, or that when the body goes for 16–17 hours without food, it enters into another state and uses fat for energy instead of carbohydrates. This affects not just the body, but the mind as well.

Alone on the Road

In 2009, I was the best climber in Norway and among the best in the world, too. But you never would have believed that if you came across me on my travels, alone in my van with just a mattress and my climbing gear for company. I had no entourage or support apparatus and I did most things myself, without an assistant or coach to plan my schedule and make arrangements before a competition.

The most important thing I had was my car, and I loved driving.

This was what it meant to be a climber: drive around and park up whenever I got tired, climb back on to my mattress, sleep, and move on when I woke up. Freedom. A kind of routine without routine, every day was different yet they all revolved around the same thing – climbing, seeking out new places and visiting friends on the scene. I'd crash with the people I visited and we'd go climbing for a few days or weeks before I moved on.

Compared with the older climbing bum's, I was still a

pretty square, scholarship-funded athlete who did something that his predecessors had never even dreamed of, namely compete in front of large audiences following a certain set of rules. I took a systematic and focused approach to my training, just like any other modern athlete. But at the same time, I craved freedom and I had a strong desire to drift around in search of the best climbing spots, and a real urge to spend time hanging out with my brothers in spirit.

Reckless Driving

In the days before I got my own license, I spent a lot of time as a passenger. All my friends liked to drive fast, especially abroad. In Spain, they goofed around in rental cars, skidding on bends to wear out the tires.

So by the time I got my own license, I was well used to fast speeds. I drove fast in France and Spain, and of course on the Autobahn highways in Germany which are notorious for their practically non-existent limits. I find that the concentration you experience at such high speeds is similar to intense climbing. You've got to hold on to the wheel and keep your gaze fixed ahead while checking the left lane for super-fast cars and keeping a close eye on your mirrors so you don't get surprised from behind.

Snapchat of Alex Honnold at Sirekrok, a crag close to Stavanger. It was an honor climbing with him. ▶

Sport climbing instead today👏🦴

Ali Hulk, 9b, Rodellar, Spain, 2010, the hardest route I have ever done. I felt light and strong.

Chapter 14

A Circus at the World Cup

By 2007, I was back to performing at a high level after my diet and came in fifth at the World Cup in mid-November, the last competition of the year. Earlier in the same season, I finished eighth at the World Championships in Aviles, France.

I loved competing and I would do it a lot between March and November. Competitions fired me up to do better and to prove myself. They also meant access and a sense of belonging to an international environment where everyone is focused on the same thing, both at the World Cup and at other events. I traveled both alone and with the Norwegian team, which often included my sister, and I liked both configurations. I got to travel often with friends from other countries, too.

I enjoyed climbing outdoors on an almost empty stomach and often I'd get by just on coffee in the mornings and cookies at lunch. But I noticed that when I ate this way at competitions, I'd end up feeling shaky and weak. My body needed more energy in that kind of high-concentration and high-performance context, so I'd take care to eat well both before and during. The extra adrenaline had me go to the restroom more often than normal.

Competitions filled me with both dread and anticipation. For weeks beforehand I would train often and hard, drawing both motivation and energy from the challenge ahead. As the event got closer, I'd take things down a notch and focus more on building up my mental and physical energy banks. I think it's important for climbers to have something in reserve and not to tire themselves out from too much intense, physical training. Moving up the wall needs to feel light and easy. Like in all other sports, it's about striking a balance between training and rest. Getting the right tension and biting point.

On arrival, I would rest up and try to gather some strength, often feeling jet-lagged in both body and mind. There would be little time to explore my new surroundings and plenty of time dedicated to rest. If things went badly, it was all too easy to doubt the point of it all.

Generally, I would sleep pretty well the night before, but the day itself could be tough. Like when the referee would come out to hang up the starting list and everyone would flock around to check their time. That always gave me a flutter in my stomach and then my nerves would start to mount.

"What am I doing this for?" I would think while waiting to be let in to climb, full of dread and anxiety. "What am I bothering with all this for?" As my turn got nearer, I'd listen to the sounds of whoever was on the wall and try to work out how high they were getting, and at the same time I'd try to remember the route after having seen it for six minutes. Those short minutes were a killer. Doubt would take hold every damn time.

But after going out and doing the first few moves, things would loosen up and my nervousness would ease away. Most of the time at least, there were also days when I would remain stiff and tense the whole time. Those were the bad days.

Isolation

The way things used to work at the World Cup was that before a competition, climbers had to go into isolation to stop them from seeing the route in advance. As of 2021, only the final and the semifinals are onsight routes.

The old system started to degenerate as more and more people took part, like when 140 people competed at Munich in 2005. The best went last and it could take up to 17 hours until it was time. So a lot of people brought sleeping bags and mattress pads to sleep or chill out in. I would often doze off on the floor while waiting for hours and hours on end.

A lot of climbers complained about being in isolation. They disliked waiting and wasting time on what felt like nothing other than sitting together in a big hall. But I liked isolation more than most people did, for several reasons. For one thing, it was a social experience. Especially in the early days, it was an opportunity to meet people I hadn't met before. I'd talk to older climbers I didn't have the nerve or the chance to speak to elsewhere and I'd get to hear what everyone else was saying. Besides that, isolation made me feel important. It meant I was part of a select group – among the best climbers in the world. That felt really great to me.

Like a Gladiator on the Wall

I liked having an audience at competitions, spectators would cheer and applaud along the way. It felt awesome. Being on the wall with thousands of eyes on me, watching every move, every second. The spectators saw everything and read your performance. The cheers and the claps felt like a nice reward for all the solitary hard work which came before.

Like on July 13 – the day before Bastille Day – every year in Chamonix, when they set off fireworks and make a big commotion before, during and after the annual competition held in the town. I felt in my element when competing in front of thousands of spectators all sitting outside, screaming and cheering from the ground below. I will always remember how great it felt to come in third at the World Cup there in 2011. That was my best placing as a senior and the same result as I got in Kranj the following year. The gap was closing between me and the top.

A Norwegian TV Hero

The pressure was doubly on at the World Championships in Arco when Norwegian TV broadcaster NRK came to make a mini documentary on me. My country was watching and I needed to bring my A game. But I wasn't worried. I liked the pressure.

On July 22, 2011, the day after the qualifiers, one of the TV crew members said:

"Fuck, blast at the Government Quarter in Oslo."

I was in my own little bubble and barely realized what

was happening. The NRK guys were getting a flood of information coming in about a bomb in downtown Oslo and then a mass-shooting on the island of Utøya – the worst terror attack in Norway's history. I called home to check that everyone was safe and thankfully they were. The next day, I wore a black mourning ribbon and finished in fourth place. My best result in a senior world championship.

The TV program on NRK in 2011 made me a household name in Norway for a short period. After more than ten years, many outside the world of climbing now knew about this intense red-headed guy from Bergen who lived partly in his car like some kind of gypsy and hauled himself up with just one finger. A feat nobody in Norway had seen before. Like some kind of circus act.

Norway's best male climber was this guy who slept and lived in his car by choice, even in the run-up to the World Championships. I stood out from other top athletes in the country who all had a huge support apparatus behind them. Most Norwegians didn't even know that types like me existed. I completely broke with their idea of athletes as these well-paid types in excellent condition. The TV show brought viewers into an unfamiliar sport and showed them what climbing competitions were like. YouTube hadn't broken into the mainstream by this stage and I wasn't active on there either. Plus, climbing still belonged to a subculture even on YouTube. It wasn't the sort of things that ordinary Norwegians had been served up on prime-time TV all that much.

Sore Loser

I didn't like doing badly and could easily lose my self-confidence. I'd ask myself: "What are you doing? Traveling half way around the world to not even make the final". Or I would think: "It's time to pack this crap in and get a proper job. No more climbing full-time, it's not going to get you anywhere".

After a bad competition, I'd feel down on myself and switch off my phone for a couple of days. My family back home would be eager for news, but I wouldn't pick up. What was I supposed to say?

Questions like "what went wrong?" or "what could you have done differently?" were easy to ask but difficult to answer.

In climbing, each competition route is new and unfamiliar, and climbers have to make their decisions in just a few split seconds. Explaining these choices in retrospect is pretty much impossible, and besides, I'd rather move on than dwell on the past. It does you no good to go digging into your mistakes.

I spoke with experts at the Norwegian Olympic Committee with experience in advising athletes facing adversity, but I didn't get much out of it. Perhaps because of my aversion to mentors and types like that. It's hard to help somebody with a negative attitude toward accepting help. No, I had to trust in myself and take responsibility. Not just wallow in self-pity.

Climbing Parties

Each World Cup always ended with a huge party in the evening. Some of the climbers were teetotalers while others would get totally wasted. For my part, I liked to join in and be involved, but I never went wild. Tomorrow would always be at the forefront of my mind. For a number of years, these parties abroad were the most important social arena in my life. All my friends belonged to this global climbing circus and among them I could cut loose. But compared to the most outgoing in this group, I remained a pretty committed athlete.

Even so, my rebellious side did come out from time to time. Like when I refused to wear the Norwegian team uniform on the podium after events, as a good Norwegian athlete was expected to do. I stood there in my normal clothes and I would get a yellow card for it. No big deal, but enough to provoke people on both sides.

World Cup, Puurs, Belgium, from the finals. I was nervous for the big dyno and fell, not able to deal with the pressure. ▶

The finals of the World Cup, Chamonix, 2014.
With nasty burns on my forearms, after having
cooked steaks in the pan and fat spilling all over.

Chapter 15

A Lean Body

All through my career, I saw myself as being too strong. I looked at my competitors and I saw small French guys with stick-thin legs, slender Italians and other lightweights with little to carry. Their bodies were well-suited for using small holds. The kind of bodies a climber should have.

Not like me. I was like a young bodybuilder or gymnast, athletic and well-proportioned. The perfect body, in the eyes of some, but I didn't see it that way. I wanted to weigh as little as possible but still to be strong.

I had chunky legs, too. Tree-trunk legs were no good to me as a climber and I desperately wanted to slim them down. But how do you get rid of muscle mass in your legs? I never trained them intentionally, but I couldn't get away without using them and so they simply refused to shrink in size.

I stopped cycling so as not to build muscle on my legs but that was about where I drew the line. I never went as far as some other climbers who would put their legs in plaster to force them down in size. Without any fractures or injuries, they would encase their legs in casts and leave them still for weeks to let the muscles shrink. I did sometimes fantasize about an injury putting my legs out of action, but I never went as far as that.

During periods of intense training, my muscles would grow and I'd be left feeling heavy and tired. If I took things easy for a while and climbed less, then my weight would go down and my body would recover. That was usually when I felt the strongest because I'd have more energy and feel a pay-off from my training.

At that time, I saw myself as being bigger than I really was. Pronounced muscles made my body look huge in the mirror, and I even hated how big my upper body looked. I had what most of my peers were desperate for – washboard abs and bulging pecs – but it just didn't count the same in the eyes of a climber. I wanted to weigh less.

I disliked my body, but I was no different to any other climber at the top. Everybody thought about their weight and wanted to minimize it. But some skinny people with less of a capacity for building muscles are naturally lighter. Four pounds less can mean a year of training or even more, which is a huge difference. It's something you need to feel in your body to understand.

There are no weight categories in climbing. A climber can be 5.4 or 6 feet tall and weigh 120 or 165 pounds. They can be scrawny or powerful, with a heavy or an explosive build. Some have raw strength, others don't. All body types compete together.

Height

I have a theory about my own height. I'm 5' 8", 5 inches shorter than my dad and just a little taller than my mom. I think that because I ate little during those last few growth years and in puberty, I didn't reach my full height. It's quite possible I was actually meant to reach 6' 1", like my dad.

I believe I actually have the size and the strength of a person that height, just compressed down into 5' 8".

Is that possible?

Well ...

Asians who move to Europe and adopt a diet which is higher in calories and richer in animal protein often grow taller compared to their parents. A high-calorie diet more easily translates into a larger body, not exclusively a heavier body. I may have put the brakes on my own development by undereating during those crucial growth years.

My mom believes that my own desire to remain fairly short also affected my growth. I was terrified that I'd grow too tall for climbing and mom thinks that through sheer will-power I somehow exerted control over my own growth.

Climbing Hungry

There are certain pictures of me where you can actually see that I must be hungry. I'm gaunt in the face with high cheekbones sticking out like crags on each side and very little meat around them. It's the sort of face that many top athletes have.

Like few others, the best climbers lose weight even when they have to perform at their best. I would eat little on those last few days before attempting a difficult route outdoors. Less and less and then almost nothing on the last three days. Right beforehand, I'd empty my bowels and try to expel as much coffee as possible. Get rid of all dead weight.

This puts body and mind in a pretty tense state. After three days with little to no food and mostly just snus and coffee for energy, as well as some inner pep ahead of the big attempt, I would become almost like a kind of beast, ready to attack. Fragile and weak from eating too little, but aggressive and eager to perform. Certainly not healthy.

My mind fully focused on each move. Starting at just a few degrees above freezing point, I would mobilize every ounce of strength in my body and often feel a warming fizz begin to spread through my limbs. My body would get warmer and it would suddenly seem as if there was nothing else in the world to do but climb and do my best in a state of complete concentration.

The Specialist, 8b+, Les Gorges du Verdon, 2016. The route was first done in 1987, an early 8b+.

Snus

I first tried snus back at Bergenshallen in 2000, aged twelve. Snus is a pouch that you place under your lip, containing tobacco, salts, water and flavors, among other things. The nicotine gets absorbed through the mucous membrane and enters straight into your blood which then pumps it around the body. It reaches the brain almost immediately, releasing a substance called dopamine which has both a calming and stimulating effect. It's addictive.

Snus is like gunpowder, with each little bag containing large amounts of nicotine. That first hit of snus knocked me so hard I could hardly move. I was supposed to go to the store with my mom afterwards, but she had to go alone that day. The first hit is the worst but as time goes on, your body builds up resistance. Snus was banned in the EU in 1992, but Sweden was granted an exemption when they joined the union in 1995. Norway was also allowed to continue selling snus.

I used snuff off and on during high school and discovered that it quelled my hunger. Instead of eating, I'd stick a pouch of snus under my lip and immediately feel better, or so it seemed anyway. In reality, it made my heart pound and it stopped my body from regaining its strengths. Once you start using snus, it becomes tough to relax without nicotine in your veins.

Snus also made it easier to keep my weight low because it boosts your metabolism. By how much is impossible to say, but I noticed the difference and felt it also affected how much water my body carried. Therein lay much of the appeal. Snus made it easier to climb well for a longer time without food. It made it easier to keep weight off and to eat more without getting too heavy. Without snus, I would need more discipline. The fact it disrupted my sleep and slowed down my body's recovery hardly seemed to matter next to everything else. Not everybody knew about it either, even if I was consuming about a box and a half a day around 2014/15. That's a lot of nicotine and a lot of little pouches.

But I only ever snussed with my feet on the ground. I never climbed with a pouch in my cheek, like some other climbers would do. I didn't want anything to distract me when climbing, so I'd wait and pop one in afterwards for a quick little kick and a calorie-free reward for my hard work.

When I eventually stopped using snus, I noticed a positive difference right away: I slept better and I had more energy. I was better off without it.

I took up coffee at the age of sixteen and although I never became addicted, I did overdo it on the coffee sometimes. It wasn't addictive in the same way as snus is and with time I even grew to like the taste.

By the bonfire, Santa Linya, February 2008. I slept in the cave for one week, in a cold sleeping bag, built for summer. From the left: Helene, me, Eric Lopez and Jens Larsen. In the back wearing blue jacket, Tomas Mrazek. Jens Larsen established and ran the climbing site 8a.nu, at the time the biggest and most important climbing site in the World.

Chapter 16

Vagabond Life

I was a professional climber for a decade from spring 2007. The freedom became a lifestyle for me, and I flunked too many subjects to pass high school. In large part because of all my absences and lack of interest for school. It felt unimportant to me, something that got in the way.

In 2010, I successfully retook geography, social studies, history and English at a private high school in Oslo to get my high school diploma and reopen the possibility to study again in the future. It seemed like a sensible thing to do although ultimately my heart wasn't in it. It would have just felt like a meaningless chore to keep showing up to classes and studying for exams, so I closed the door on my studies. I was well into my climbing career and I didn't want to have a plan B in life. I wanted to put everything into climbing.

My dad said I should study past high school, but he and my mom gave us kids free rein to choose our own paths in life. He is a professor of political science at Bergen University and naturally interested in theoretical learning. But not me.

Sasha

I lived for climbing as a teenager and didn't chase after girls. It was difficult to imagine even having a girlfriend who did anything other than climb.

A Christmas in Spain I met American climber Sasha DiGulian. She was good-looking and we discovered right away that there was chemistry between us. Talking came easy and we had a shared passion in climbing. She was among the best in her country and still lived at home with her parents in Washington, D.C.

We started going out and suddenly everything was different.

I went from being a solitary climbing monk to a guy with a girlfriend. It was my first proper relationship, and that meant another person to take into consideration. As per usual, I became absorbed by the relationship. Just like with everything else, there is no middle ground for me. Sasha became the focus of all my attention and the center of my world, even if much of my life remained private.

Talking about girlfriends or being in love was not something I really did with my family in Norway. It wasn't a subject we discussed at the dinner table and so I kept most of that stuff to myself, just like a lot of young men do. In that sense I was a pretty typical introverted Norwegian kid, but that's how I wanted to be. My family and friends knew that I liked to keep my private life private.

Being in a relationship introduced me to new sides of life. Sasha not only brought me into a new world, but into a new country and culture, different from what I knew back in Norway. Her life was right at the political center of the United States, in a city where her parents rubbed shoulders with many prominent people. Climbing really could open some incredible doors, both to new people and new places.

For periods I lived with Sasha and was based in the US. Washington, D.C. was not the best city for a climber, but I wanted to be together with Sasha as much as possible and we could see a real future together. Pretty soon we started thinking long-term, just like many young couples do in their first serious relationship. We were like most kids our age, totally captivated by our feelings for one another.

We even joked about getting married in Las Vegas one day, when we were driving home from the gym. If nothing else, it would have made my residency situation a lot easier.

Back then I truly believed that Sasha and I could be together for the rest of our lives. But we were immature in our own way. We had traveled a lot and gotten by just fine abroad, and we were well-experienced in these kinds of things for our age, but unused to being in such a close relationship.

While in D.C. I continued with the lifestyle I knew, going to a climbing gym in the mornings to climb and to train. But having a girlfriend affected my climbing. Our relationship drew away energy and attention and meant I was no longer focused on just the one thing. In many ways this was great, and I was happy in a new and unfamiliar way. I felt somehow more grown up even if I wasn't really, and I was accepted into her family who treated me really well and threw their support behind me.

Burglary in Italy

One day in summer, Sasha and I went climbing in Arco and we parked our car several hundred yards away. A few hours later, we returned to find that the driver seat window had been smashed in. A lot was left behind, but they swiped our credit cards which were pretty much the most important things we had with us. The next morning, we went down to the police station in town to report the theft but the police said they couldn't help us.

What were two young tourists to do?

Sasha knew the American ambassador in Bern, Switzerland. He was a family friend, so we drove there and when we arrived, armed guards swept our car for explosives. Getting into the ambassador's residence was a serious deal, and staying the night wasn't ordinarily allowed.

But being friends of the ambassador, Sasha and I got the five-star treatment.

"What would you like to eat" asked a waiter.

Our requests were laid down in front of us.

I was shown to a bedroom where I was told former president George Bush had once spent the night. And Oprah Winfrey too, but not at the same time, of course. It's not every young Norwegian guy who gets to enjoy hospitality like that in such beautiful surroundings.

Sasha and I were together for two and a half years. At first everything was awesome and we simply floated along on a wave of our own emotions. "We're not made to argue," I thought, fully convinced.

But after a year and a half we did start to fight. Little at first, then more. Things became more complicated. We noticed that we were different. I wanted to spend more time climbing in Europe. Being far away from each other and coming from different countries only reinforced our differences, and we decided to break up. Sasha became one of the best female climbers in the world.

Beloved Spain

Ever since that first trip back in 2003, I've visited Spain so many times that it's hard to remember what happened which time. I've made dozens of trips of varying durations.

My days there were glorious. I'd sleep until nine in the morning, eat a leisurely breakfast or no breakfast at all, sometimes watch a climbing film and then head out to the crag for the rest of the day, where we'd climb until it got dark. It always felt good to come back to our rental home and cook some dinner or relax after seven to eight hours in the fresh air, almost like a working day that uses every muscle in the body. We hiked lots too, putting our legs to good use. If we were celebrating something, like finishing a project, I'd drink wine.

I always looked forward to our dinners. I would eat a lot and really enjoy the food, which always tasted better after those long days beneath the wide open sky.

There were always new routes to try in Spain. I enjoyed starting on a new project. Getting a little farther with each passing day. I'd memorize the routes and through them in the evening, picturing them in my mind's eye. Maybe 120 moves for the hands and feet, all in order.

Sometimes I'd lie in bed back in Norway and think about Spanish routes I was yet to complete, thousands of miles away. Carefully weighing up each and every move. It can take several weeks or months to master a route, and success is never guaranteed. I'd dream about routes too and often visualize myself on the wall.

Climbers do things this way and there are often few witnesses to great achievements. Preferably just one friend safe and sound down there, possibly a few others, when climbing difficult routes. There were no cheers or awards for completing difficult routes, and no prize money either. Others had to simply trust that you were telling the truth when you logged an achievement online.

Because difficult routes commanded high status and are so rewarding both physically and mentally, free from the stress of competition, many top climbers prioritized that over the World Cup. This didn't make them any less professional and they were still sponsored by climbing brands and other companies because they were doing something spectacular which could be photographed and featured in magazines. This was still in the days before social media. Once they came along, it was left more up to the individual climber to drum up as much attention as possible around their climbing.

Ali Hulk

Ali Hulk is a 9b route in Rodellar, Spain. I went there in summer 2010 to start working on it. I practiced its 84 moves, breaking it up into individual sections and becoming more and more familiar with the route. I fell several times per day on the crux, probably about a hundred times in total. Fairly standard on such a tough route. The key was to try again and to not lose heart.

I went over the moves in my head and memorized them. Including foot placements, there were a few hundred in total. I'd continue like this for a while, feeling more and more ready to go all out. Filled with both dread and anticipation before the big day. It's important to psych yourself up beforehand and to understand that you're doing something tough and physically demanding. Something which takes strength, mental energy and concentration. For me, it felt almost like going to war.

After a month of preparation, the day came.

I was feeling psyched and ready. I checked the weather forecast and made sure the skin on my fingers was in good enough condition. The best time to go climbing in Spain is in the winter. Summers are too hot. Sunny weather means sweat from both fingers and the rock. I prefer cool and overcast weather with little wind and clouds in the sky. In Rodellar it is only possible to climb in Summer. It is too wet rest of the year.

I completed Ali Hulk on August 19, 2010. A 9b. It was a huge deal for me.

It was such a relief to finish the project and scrub all those moves from my memory. They served no purpose anymore, so I let them go. Some people still remember all the moves from previous routes down to the smallest details, but I preferred to move on towards new goals.

We had to swim to Picinetta, a climbing area in Rodellar. This was just before my onsight of Cosi Fan Tutte in 2013. The water was freezing cold, and my body fat was low. I had never before been this cold.

*Onsighting Cosi Fan Tutte,
8c+. Photo taken on the top,
just before the crux.*

Neanderthal

Chris Sharma did a route called *Neanderthal* near Santa Linya in 2007. For a while it was considered the world's most difficult.

I wanted to do it and went down to try it for the first time in 2011. I was on one of my regular trips to Spain which lasted until April. Conditions are often wet and unfavorable on that route and you need to wait for dry weather before you can give it a go. I tried it over several seasons and fell at least 50 times on the crux. Where Chris could cram in three fingers in his own strange way, I managed only two. He willingly shared all his beta. Me, the little shy Norwegian kid from the café, actually managed to speak with my childhood idol this time around.

For years I worked on the route, occasionally traveling back to Norway to train and relax. It helped to train and to get away from those peaceful Spanish surroundings, to see family and friends back in Norway. Hit up some intense sessions in the climbing gym and then fly back down to Barcelona to try again. A continuously repeating cycle. The more and the longer I worked on the route, the more determined I became to complete it. I even shred down to about 135 pounds to give myself an edge. My mood suffered from eating so little and I felt my energy drain away.

I spent spring 2013 working on *Neanderthal*. The route gets its name from the fact that Neanderthals once lived in the cave and in the others nearby. It was cool to imagine them. How they slept and cooked meat over the fire, living in their own way some 40,000 years ago.

I would often think about those people and their way of life while waiting in the cave, wrapped up in lots of clothes. This continued for weeks without success and I simply couldn't get the route out of my mind. I just wanted to get it done so I could move on to something else. But I never did manage to complete Neanderthal.

It was a defeat.

On April 17, 2013, four of us set off to Picineta, a few hours walk along and partly through a river – there was me, Henning Wang, his brother, and Ragnhild Eriksrud. Four Norwegians looking for a place off the beaten track. Literally swimming against the current. I had little fat on my body and felt freezing cold in the water. In total, the journey there took a couple of hours.

I warmed myself up on an 8a and felt pretty good. I felt better than ever, so I decided to try to onsight the route *Cosi Fan Tutte*, although I wasn't hot on my chances.
The route is about 200 feet long and graded 8c+. The first part came easy enough, and I breezed through the first 150 feet. When was the crux? It came around the last 20 feet, when the sun beamed down and made it extra hard to see the holds and find a solution. I thought about a time I fell when onsighting a route in Spain and got so pissed off that I hurled my climbing shoes into the forest, never to find them again. I was determined not to fall and miss another chance to onsight a route, because you only get one shot. Falling felt like a real possibility on more than a couple of the moves.

But in the end, I clipped the anchor at the top of *Cosi Fan Tutte* and became the fifth person in the world to onsight an 8c+. It felt amazing. For me, this was even bigger than doing another 9b. It made up for the fact I never managed the *Neanderthal*.

Spanish Clubbing and New Vices

Some weekends in Spain, we would drive from Santa Linya to Barcelona to go out. Rather than to book accommodation, we'd stay out really late like the Spaniards, who often don't even get to the club until two or three in the morning and then party until sunrise.

We swapped tranquil surroundings for the buzz of the city. It was a stark contrast to go from hanging off a wall or sitting on a folding chair in the countryside to a nightclub pumping out loud music and swarming with girls. Us climbers felt a bit like cavemen visiting the city. The journey into the city had an intoxicating effect on us, with all its crowds and lights, its loud music and new sounds. We would drink and join in the fun. Because the party didn't end until well into the next day, we would sleep on the beach rather than check into a hostel.

I smoked marijuana for the first time in Alquezar around 2007/08. I was sitting in a house that the guys were renting, took a few drags and felt no effect. What was the point in this? I thought to myself and toked a little more. Half an hour went by, smoking in silence and sitting in a chair.

Suddenly it hit me like a ton of bricks. The weed began to

take effect and my heart started to pound, as if it were going to explode. It was a frightening sensation and my heart rate monitor was showing 160 beats per minute. I felt almost paralyzed, but clear-headed, and sensible enough to realize:

"I need to go up and lie down in my room."

I got up and staggered over to the stairs, taking each step on unsteady legs. Going through the doorway into my room in this creaky old house from the 17th century, I saw my bed like a mirage in the desert and thought: "there!"

I lurched over but suddenly my head was vibrating and the room was spinning. I fell to the floor and knocked my head, one hand just about on the bed. I slept like that the whole night and woke up in the same position the next morning, with a huge bump on my head. But fresh and headache-free after a good night's sleep.

I smoked a few more times after that but I never took it up, in part because I also noticed how it made others lethargic. Addictions come easy to me and I didn't want to become hooked on weed. It was enough simply to try, and I've never touched any form of synthetic drugs. After flirting briefly with smoking, I decided I would stick to alcohol. It left me with a headache the next day, but at least it was a more familiar and predictable form of intoxication.

Neanderthal 9b, Santa Linya,
2013, after falling on the crux.
I pulled myself up using the
rope and continued to the top.

On our way back from Picineta. I was on a down after having given up on Neanderthal the day before, but onsighting Cosi Fan Tutte is still one of my proudest moments.

Chapter 17

Restless?

It's been said that I'm a restless type. Restless is a word with plenty of synonyms. In my Norwegian dictionary, the first three which pop up alphabetically, roughly translated, are: "anxious, worried, unquiet." The last two are: "nervy and insecure".

It makes me wonder, what is actually meant by restless? No way am I anxious or insecure. Maybe unquiet in the sense that I like to do stuff and to be in motion. To be moving forward. My grandfather John Midtbø was like that, always moving about, changing jobs and taking on new challenges. People tell me I remind them of him.

Many young men are labelled as restless or unquiet. That's because their bodies are built for movement and physical development, but they grow up in a society where children are expected to sit indoors during the day, learning theory. They're shuffled about by bus, placed in a room and told to sit – against their instincts – sometimes even in bad-quality air. Even though this is happening on a massive scale all over the world, it hasn't been ongoing for decades and decades. But its impact has been felt, leaving many in poorer shape, with less strength and less mobility. And the change has come fast.

I grew up before most Norwegian kids became almost permanently connected to their phones and computers, and that's part of the reason I had so much freedom growing up.

In the old days, a driven kid like me would have been sent out to do manual labor rather than spend their time climbing or becoming an athlete. I might have become a sailor, a lumberjack or a navvy if I'd grown up in the 19th century. As a kid, I built cabins out of wood near our house in Bergen. There are still planks and logs to be found where I grew up.

For me, climbing was an outlet for all the energy and drive I had. You could see it as a kind of inner turmoil and sometimes that's what it is. But not always. In any case, getting to visit new places, meet new people and see new things was something extra that came with climbing, something an ordinary job would never have brought me. There was no work in the world that could have given me everything I wanted.

The actual reality of work is something I know very little about. The only real job I ever had was selling newspapers at the weekend from time to time, back when I was ten. I grew up free from ordinary obligations like that. Most kids in Norway work summer jobs or pick up odd jobs after school, mowing lawns for the neighbors or working the check out in shops to earn a few extra bucks. But not me. Climbing took up all my time and energy and meant I was traveling for months each year, even over the summer break. Clocking up 250 days abroad a year left zero time to work. Climbing became both an enjoyable job and an all-consuming hobby which then merged into a lifestyle. In that sense, I was privileged and some people thought of me as a spoilt kid from a rich country. But that's not how I felt. My family wasn't loaded and we lived within our means.

Arrogant?

I didn't like talking about climbing with outsiders and I would get irritated if they asked me questions, even just to be polite. They didn't get it. But because there were periods in my life when climbing was all I thought about, those questions were pretty much the only way to reach me. Even so, I only wanted to talk about climbing with other climbers and not people on the outside who didn't know how the sport worked.

My strong will took me far. It was necessary, too, in order to compete with the steady stream of new recruits coming out of solid climbing nations. But being stubborn isn't always smart.

Athletes often have a lot they need to learn, and the trick is figuring out what suits best. A good coach could surely have helped me reach the podium at the World Cup even more times and to win medals at the Senior World Championships. But I was not at all open to advice and no doubt lost out as a result.

I took the responsibility myself and blamed no one else.

It's important to trust your own assessments and to form your own opinions as a top athlete. In retrospect, it's easy to regret stuff because you grow wiser and learn more with time, but by then it's too late. With my personality and nature being the way they are, I can't imagine having done things much differently in my climbing career.

Hanshelleren, Flatanger. I am standing on the rock formation, that according to the saying, was the troll "Hans". He was about to get it on with the troll wife, but froze in the meeting of the sun.

*Hanshelleren, Flatanger, 2012. Me to the left
and Christoph Frutiger to the right.*

Chapter 18

Hanshelleren and Adam Ondra

Hanshelleren is what's known in Norwegian as a heller – a cave-like rock formation with an overhang that keeps the interior dry, making it a suitable place to spend the night and store your things. It's located in the rocky coastal region of Flatanger, carved out by dramatic waves from the high seas. Once inhabited by cave people, it is now home to the world's most difficult climbs.

A couple of routes were bolted around the cave many years ago, but on the sides where it's less steep. And it was only a handful of routes.

Myself and several others had heard about Hanshelleren and wanted to check it out. In 2010, Eirik Birkelund Olsen and I set off from Stavanger in the south of Norway on a 20-hour-long road trip up to Flatanger. Daniel Andrada, French route setter Laurent Laporte and a friend traveled there by plane at the same time. We rented a house in Lauvsnes with an ambition to bolt some of the world's most difficult routes.

The local farmer wanted to attract climbers to the area and boost tourism, and they were very keen for us to bolt new routes. The Norwegian Bolt Foundation and Runar Carlsen paid us a small sum for the job and supplied us with bolts, which could get to be quite expensive if you needed a lot.

Hanshelleren is an enormous cave and difficult to describe. We scoped it out and looked for natural lines. We chose four different routes to bolt. Mine was called *Thor's Hammer*. The others were named *Eye of Odin*, *Nordic Flower* and *Muy Verde*.

I spent a full week of bolting, without getting it done. To bolt in Hanshelleren is physical demanding, and I had to return back later to finish bolting the about 500 feet long route. I thought Thor's Hammer to be 9b.

Then the others and I started spreading the word about our new and difficult routes in Hanshelleren. Adam Ondra decided to try his hand in 2012. At the annual bouldering competition in Voss, Adam wanted to swing by on his way to Flatanger.

The first time I ran into him was at the Youth Cup in Brno, his hometown in Czechia. That was around 2002 and he was too young to take part, but already recognized as a wunderkind in the sport. He was a so-called demo climber and he cried in disappointment when he fell. It made an impression. We all saw how much and how hard he tried.

In 2012, Adam was among the best climbers in the world. So it was just sensational that he wanted to come all the way to Voss, a small Norwegian town on the edge of the world.

Adam traveled to Voss in car with his photographer and manager in tow – a whole support apparatus. Surprisingly I won the whole competition, which was cool for our home crowd. I don't think Adam took the defeat badly and he remained upbeat.

He went on to Matre in Hordaland afterward, one of the places with most rainfall in Norway, to try a boulder problem called *Blood Redemption* – the hardest in Norway, at that time an 8C. My hardest boulder and first ascent. He got it on day one, like an act of small revenge for the bouldering competition the day before. I'd spent weeks working on *Blood Redemption*. Adam suggested a downgrade to 8B+.

He went on to Flatanger and sent me a text:

"Can I do *Thor's Hammer*?"

"Of course," I answered.

Adam did it and put it as 9a+. I had thought 9b.

A few months later he did *Change* and suggested that to be 9b+. He returned to Flatanger the next year and bolted a route which he named *Silence*. It's about 150 feet long and features several difficult passages, starting with about 60 feet of steep climbing at 8b level, then several isolated extremely hard boulder problems.

Adam traveled to Flatanger seven times over the next few years to work on *Silence*. The ten hardest moves in the three cruxes took him four weeks to put together. He even got help from a physiotherapist to train and strengthen his body for the very particular movements he needed to make if he were to climb *Silence*. He finally did it on September 3, 2017, the world's first 9c. And the most difficult on the planet to date.

Bolting of Thor's Hammer, Flatanger, 2012, at the start of the route. It's impossible to rappel down from the top, it's too steep. When I dropped equipment, I had to rappel to the ground and jumar back up.

Blood Redemption, 8B+, Matre, 2010. The boulder that Adam Ondra sent in 2012.

Chapter 19

Oslo Nightlife

Around 2014, I started to get tired of life as a climber. The draw was wearing off and I no longer felt the same drive to travel for competitions and to throw everything I had at the sport. I was still performing well and I was still among the best in the world, but I wasn't improving. Fourth place at the World Championships in 2011 was my best result, plus third place in Colombia at the World Games in 2013. The sport was developing and the talent rising.

An obsession that had lasted 15 years was now beginning to fade after several weekends of poor results. Climbing was fun, yes, and I loved traveling and climbing outdoors, but the intense commitment and constant focus on competitions was starting to grate on me. Hardly surprising, I guess. Everything has its time.

Out of season, I started partying more at home in Oslo. I would go out with my friends to clubs downtown and elsewhere to drink and meet girls. It was a strange and unfamiliar world at first. Climbing parties were usually just boys or men and we mostly talked about climbing. When we got drunk, we'd take ourselves up lamp posts and do other shit like that. We were together in our own bubble, either here in Norway or among friends from other countries.

Going out in Oslo was a whole new world for me. I would drink, meet girls and plug in to what was a pretty normal way of life for most guys in their twenties. I liked it. It felt like I was finally making up for all the things I missed out on in my teenage years. Though I hated the hangovers on Sunday mornings and would often swear to start taking it easy, even if the next weekend would often be more of the same. But I didn't go out partying every weekend and took things easy during competition season, when I'd be traveling a lot.

My partying days came around the same time I started using Instagram, which took up time and proved a distraction from other things in my life. Climbing included. I was glad it didn't exist sooner in my career. It would have diverted too much attention from climbing and training.

Around the same time, Norway was announced as the host of the World Cup, which would be held at the Sørmarka Arena in Stavanger in 2015. This was the first time that a country in Scandinavia had hosted the event, and for a country like Norway to be given the honor was a huge deal. It meant a huge opportunity for upcoming Norwegian climbers and plenty of motivation to train extra hard and climb with the greats right here on home turf. But the buzz wasn't enough. Eight climbers qualified for the finals, I was number nine. I swore to myself that this would be my last big competition.

I continued climbing full time and living on sponsorship money from Norrøna and Five Ten, and on my grant from the Norwegian Olympic Committee. Financially, I was doing just fine. I felt free and lived alone in a big apartment by Bislett Stadium for six years on and off between 2011 and 2017.

Speeches and Shares

Another source of income was public speaking, even if it was hell for me to get up and talk in front of people. I hated giving presentations at school and even just doing ice-breakers at team gatherings would cause me a little anguish. I'd get nervous and the words just wouldn't flow.

My first public speaking request came in 2009, from a small town called Torviksbukt which was opening a new climbing wall. They offered me a huge sum of $2000 for one talk – a small fortune for a guy like me, just to open my mouth on a subject I loved. It was an offer I simply couldn't turn down. Famous people and sports personalities are often offered this kind of work, if for nothing else than to be seen and heard on their own terms.

I felt a nervousness bubble up within me, almost to boiling point. Magnus from Bergen giving a talk. The guy who never takes orders from anybody doing something against his will. The time was approaching and I could feel my chest getting tighter. There was no other way – I needed a drop of alcohol. And at a Christian folk high school no less. I downed two bottles of beer in a back room and hid the evidence well out of sight. It would not be a good look to get caught drinking alcohol at a Christian folk high school before a talk. And I hadn't even cultivated a taste for beer yet, so those two lukewarm bottles tasted pretty much like piss.

The 30 to 40 people in my audience sat politely and listened, looking at my pictures which for them seemed like images from a world of adventures. It was an experience for them and an insight into the everyday life and existence of a professional climber. In the end, I gave a good and interesting talk without once looking at any of the faces in the semi-darkened hall. Giving speeches turned out to be pretty tame and it was actually quite rewarding to share knowledge that others wanted to hear.

I learned how to speak in front of an audience but even so I didn't give all that many talks. I felt more comfortable on social media, equipped with a camera and the opportunity to edit. Plus, that way I could reach thousands of people at once and in a totally different way compared to a live audience.

From around 2014, I started to develop an interest in stocks and I began trading on the Oslo Stock Exchange. Often, I'd hold stocks for just a short time before selling them on. I read the financial dailies and followed developments and trends in the market. I could feel myself beginning to get sucked deeper and deeper in and stock valuations gradually stole focus away from my climbing. Just like with everything else in life, I took stock trading seriously and went at it with full determination.

I traded in small sums at first and thought I was an

expert. I was in the green for several years and I believed my returns were the result of a natural flair. But in reality it was all down to fluke. I knew too little about the market and I was kind of naïve. But even so, it was an educational experience and I soon realized that short-term trading on the Oslo Stock Exchange was not for me.

Trolltunga

In summer 2016, German Jan Vincent Kleine and I went to the famous Trolltunga rock formation in Tyssedal, south-east of Bergen. The name means troll's tongue because the rocky outcrop literally looks like a tongue sticking out over the water below. We started walking late at night in fog and drizzle arriving at around two in the morning with no tourists in sight, just a city of tents. Everyone was asleep. There were some bolts there, so I hitched a rope to a bolt and rappelled down to look for places to climb.

Jan Vincent took some pictures of me which looked both spectacular and insanely scary. But I was wearing a harness and rope, so there was no danger, and I mentioned this in the caption I wrote before posting to Instagram.

The picture spread like wildfire and got loads of likes. NRK called and I gave them permission to republish it – again, to all kinds of different reactions.

Some people thought what I was doing looked reckless and they responded with anger, which is a natural reaction when something looks scary. People would say things like "I don't want my taxes being wasted on saving him if he has an accident" and so on. But if I had fallen, there's no doubt I would have died. That's why I was wearing a rope and harness. Even the local police released a statement.

For me, it felt just typical that people were reacting to something outside the actual sport itself, to something other than what I was actually engaged in.

Some people warned me that the Trolltunga picture was setting a bad example that others might try and copy. But I don't buy that argument.

Few people rush out and start tearing up the streets in their cars because they watched a Formula One race on TV. Most people know their limits. In the same way, I don't think the 2018 film *Free Solo* about Alex Honnold did much to recruit people to free solo. If anything, it was more like a warning against getting involved.

The three of us all met up the next week: Jan Vincent, Alex and I, after the photographer had spliced us all together beforehand.

Alex Honnold and Øgletrynet
Alex was in France and flew to Stavanger one rainy day. Typical West Norway weather. The two of us had never met, but we knew all about each other.

I noticed right away that Alex is like most young men and down to earth. We drove to Lysefjorden to climb a route called *Mamma* on Kjerag, but it rained and climbing was impossible. We spent the night in a cabin and waited in vain. It was going to take several days or even weeks before the wall would be dry enough, so we drove back up to Bergen and more familiar climbing turf. Ironically enough, Bergen was one of the few places in the country where it wasn't actually raining at that time.

I had previously done *Øgletrynet* 8a, at the age of thirteen and the two of us decided to try it again. The idea of climbing free solo entered my mind on the way there, perhaps after doing the route at least four times with a rope. Alex easily managed to do the most difficult part with a rope, but not easily enough and so I snuffed the idea of trying it free solo. We talked about it and I wanted to do it properly, meaning without mats underneath.

Free soloing is something unfamiliar to me. It makes me feel out of control. My whole body goes tense and I need to use so much extra energy, totally unlike Alex who climbs in a state of zen relaxation.

I spent that whole day psyching myself up to do *Øgletrynet* without a rope. My fingers would need to be totally dry and my skin perfect. The whole route is just 45 feet and the crux comes after about the first 15 or 20. From then on it's relatively easy.

I started and I thought to myself: If things don't feel right after the first four or five moves, then I'll hop down. After a few seconds I got what's known as Elvis leg. Uncontrolled up-and-down movements in my feet which climbers sometimes experience in these situations. But despite that, I got off to a good start and soon reached the crux. I thought to myself: If I fall there and kick off the rock into some bushes, then I might get away with little more than a twisted ankle. That wouldn't be so bad.

I got past the crux and had to keep going. There was no way back. I took a deep breath, knuckled down and managed to complete the route. I felt an enormous relief when I got to the top – it gave me a real buzz that lasted for days. It felt like a real special experience, and with none other than Alex Honnold watching silently on from the ground and Jan Vincent harnessed up and taking photographs. I was pretty satisfied with the day, especially considering that my form really wasn't at its best.

Later, Alex and I did an 8a on the island of Syltøy, a technically challenging route about 90 feet long that we did with a rope. Alex surprised me by saying he could have free soloed it. I would never even have considered the possibility. It was too difficult and technical.

The environmental activist and minimalist in Alex shone through during our time together. He often wore the same clothes and ate mostly organic food. He would eat meat but only from animals that had been treated well. At one point we lost a sling when climbing, so afterwards Alex scaled a back route to go up and get it. So much energy had gone into producing it, he said, so it wouldn't be right to leave it behind.

My last World Cup, Stavanger, 2015.

Free soloing Øgletrynet in 2016, that was my first 8a back in 2002. This is just past the crux, near the top of the 45 feet long route. Alex Honnold on the ground.

Trolltunga, the Troll tongue, at night, summer 2016. We were going to pick Alex Honnold up at the airport and checked Trolltunga out on the way there.

Chapter 20

The Olympics

In 2016, I was frustrated. I wasn't keeping up with developments in the sport and I was starting to think about the future. One day that year, I was sitting in a café near my home in Oslo, together with Stian Christophersen from the Norwegian Climbing Association. "What is going to become of me?" I asked in a rare moment of uncertainty.

"What am I going to do in the future?" Christophersen encouraged and reassured me. I figured there would be opportunities to make a living from climbing, to set routes and do stuff related to the sport. After all, it was still on the rise.

Soon came the news that climbing was going to be a sport in the Tokyo Olympics in 2020.

A lot of people told me I had to stay in the game. "Don't give up now".

Going to the Olympics had never been a dream of mine. It was a distant concept and the thought of taking part didn't give me butterflies in my stomach or fill me with energy and motivation.

Even so, I accepted when the Olympic Committee offered me a place in the training group in 2016. Third place at the World Games in 2013 came with a scholarship of $8000. Coming under the wing of the Olympic Committee meant access to their facilities in the tranquil Sognsvann area north of Oslo: training areas, canteen, doctor, physiotherapist, hotel, dietary guidance and more. Not the kind of offer you can easily turn down.

I was the only Norwegian candidate in climbing. All athletes had to qualify and compete internationally for 20 spots, regardless of level, so even just getting into the Games was difficult.

The way climbing was to be organized at the Olympics meant there would be one winner within a combination of bouldering, lead climbing and speed climbing in pairs, the latter being something that neither I nor most of the other competitors had trained in. This kind of climbing was particularly well developed in Russia where competitors climb standardized routes free from technical challenges. The idea is to just haul yourself up with virtually zero thought for problem solving. The IOC felt that this competition format would work well on television.

I liked the Olympic Committee and they treated me well. All I had to do was contact them and they would fix me up with a doctor's appointment or a physiotherapy session in next to no time. They arranged for me to do a DXA body scan which detected that I had about half a pound less muscle mass in my left arm, which explained why it was a little weaker. I did some targeted training to fix the problem and saw in my next DXA scan that the two arms had evened out.

The same scan also measures the body's fat percentage although with a certain margin of error. I was eleven percent and 150 pounds out of season. My competition weight was a few pounds lighter with a fat percentage closer to eight.

The Olympic Committee advised me to give up coffee and start taking caffeine tablets instead. One cup of coffee contains an indeterminable amount of caffeine while tablets contain a precise dose. I started taking the pills in the morning but stopped before long. Coffee just tasted too good.

They also recommended that I start drinking beetroot juice too, as it helps the body get rid of lactic acid.

A third suggestion was to take creatine supplements to help my body endure more training, but I didn't even start with those. The Olympic Committee's advice was good and well-meaning, but they couldn't see the wood for the trees.

"Midtbø quits," read a headline in the Norwegian press in May 2017.

My career as a competitive climber was over. I didn't have the energy for it anymore. I enjoyed training and I was motivated to work out, but the hunger was gone – that trembling hunger that an athlete simply needs if they are going to reach the top. The fire in my belly had gone out, so whether or not I still enjoyed training was now beside the point.

What was I to do?

I had no qualifications beyond high school, besides of

course from the school of life. I was renting my house and I was a bachelor, albeit debt-free and with money in the bank. I had saved all throughout my career because I'm frugal by nature. Having some money behind you provides a safety net and the opportunity to invest. In 2017, I was involved in what was a very important project for me.

For about three years before, Frictionwalls and I had been wanting to open a climbing gym in Oslo. But it was difficult to find a space large enough and investors were skeptical. It was proving tough to find someone willing to split the risk. We got in contact with businessman Anders Opsal who was interested in opening a climbing center himself and we agreed to rent his premises and run the facility. On April 1, 2017 we were finally able to open Oslo Klatresenter.

I invested all of my savings into the project and hoped that my share, 7.5 percent, would be enough to live from. Plus, I could work there and continue with my old lifestyle of climbing and traveling without needing another job. That was the goal. I wanted to live like before.

Chapter 21

Social Media

YouTube wasn't around when I was a kid. It launched in 2004 when I was 16. But it wasn't until around 2014 that I started watching videos on there. I mostly enjoyed watching documentary style videos because I thought they were interesting and a good way to learn new stuff.

In 2014, one of my sponsors, Norrøna, thought that I should start using Instagram, but I didn't see the point since I was already active on Facebook. In any case, I posted some photos and training videos on Instagram and was surprised by how well they did.

My first few posts on Instagram were just climbing photos that I thought were cool. Nobody paid much attention, that kind of content was everywhere. My bare-chested training videos got more traction, so I posted more and some got several hundred thousand views. I developed a sense for what people wanted to see and adapted my posts. Dedicated climbers often disliked what I was doing. They saw it as selling out to promote something other than climbing, and I could totally get where they were coming from. I used to hold the exact same opinion.

YouTube

One evening in 2016, I was sitting in my apartment in Oslo together with my sister Hannah. She'd just broken up with her boyfriend and moved in with her big brother. She was watching a reality TV show called *Bloggerne*, about people in Norway who blog and do social media.

"You could do that, Magnus," she said.

No way, not blogging. But vlogging on YouTube, maybe.

Spontaneously, I posted a request on Instagram asking if anybody could film and edit videos. Several replies came in and I chose 19-year-old Robin Norbotten from Vestfold, south of Oslo, whose sole experience was endless hours watching YouTube videos. I figured it was smart to work with somebody young who understood the medium and how it works.

The apartment in Oslo belonged to family and they wanted to sell. After more than six years in a favorable lease, it was time to move out onto a hot property market. I didn't have the money to buy someplace similar in the city, so I bought a house in Østfold, about an hour away from the downtown area. I moved there in March 2017 with plans to spruce the place up and start working on YouTube at the same time. Robin moved in as well so that we could make videos together.

Because I had 100,000 followers on Instagram, I thought it would be easy to get them on YouTube too. But that wasn't the case. Instagram was more training videos, whereas YouTube was more of a vlog, where we filmed everything we did.

A lot was happening all at the same time.

I was doing up my house, training for the Olympics,

starting up my YouTube channel and working at Oslo Klatresenter.

Robin and I spent a lot of time making videos, between about 10 and 25 minutes long, but we weren't getting the response we were after. We went to Arco to film some videos there and in May 2017, I sent an email to Nicki Horak at the Norwegian Climbing Association to drop out of the Olympics. By this stage, they'd already figured.

Robin and I made 49 videos together without managing to really get things off the ground. We ended our collaboration in July 2017. I kept going on my own, but it was hard to work so much without getting anything back for all those hours put in.

By March–April 2018, I was ready to give up the channel and I stopped posting for a while. Should I just pack the whole YouTube thing in?

With Tom and Juji in the USA
On July 29, 2018, I got an email from Tom Boyden in Charlotte, North Carolina. He knew me as a climber and wanted to make a video about grip strength for their YouTube channel, Jujimufu. Juji's real name is Jon Call and he has a private gym in his garage just outside Charlotte. Back then they were putting out three videos a week.

Just before contacting me, they had made a video about grip strength featuring unknown climbers and it went viral – I'd seen it myself, and he wanted to do a follow-up with a famous climber. First they asked Alex Honnold and

Alexander Megos, who either came back with a no or said they were unavailable. I was their third choice and I said yes right away. Juji and Tom paid for my ticket and I flew to Charlotte via New York on September 1, 2018.

Tom Boyden picked me up at the airport and we drove back to his apartment to get started. We had zero downtime that day or any other day after that until I left.

"Eat breakfast now," Tom said the next morning as I lay on the couch in his shack. "We won't have time to eat anything until tonight".

Rather than skip breakfast like I usually would, I dug in and followed their fast-pace program, recording twelve videos over four days, three for me and nine for their channel. Tom planned everything. As well as recording, he edited everything and hardly slept a wink during my whole visit. That's how he worked a lot of the time.

The grip-strength video got hundreds of thousands of views and went viral right away. Tom recommended my channel and I went from 40,000 subscribers to 100,000 in just a week. All of a sudden my channel was growing and so were my earnings. Viewers were subscribing from all over the world.

Tom is one of those fun guys who always seems to be at the center of everything. I liked hanging out with him, all according to Tom's plan.

He could get angry and often bickered with Juji – they were like an old married couple sometimes. The fast pace, the lack of sleep and the long days all took their toll on his mood.

But I liked him and I learned a lot about YouTube and the craft they practiced. Tom genuinely cared about me and he wanted my channel to grow.

Juji was another character. He became famous on the eleventh season of America's Got Talent for doing the splits across two chairs while holding a barbell over his head. Another video that went viral.

He started training at the age of thirteen and practiced a discipline known as tricking – difficult jumps and flips in real-world settings, like a garden, the street or between buildings. In later years, he took up powerlifting and bodybuilding but without losing his soft side. Taekwondo, too. All that combined with humor and wisdom is what makes the Jujimufu brand, now a well-known figure on YouTube and social media. He also wrote a training book called *Legendary Flexibility* which was soon followed by a series of others. From December 2016 onward, he was making his living entirely from the fitness industry.

I saw how Juji ate six times a day. All his meals came from boxes and were eaten at regular points in the day without any time going to waste. As much as possible in precise doses finely balanced between carbohydrates, fats and proteins. It was the opposite of my approach, which was still to eat as little as possible and to often go several hours without anything at all. We were an odd pair, him a ravenous fitness type and bodybuilder and me a climber fueled by coffee and who had just given up snus.

I visited Tom and Juji five times in 2018, 2019 and the

year after. My last visit ended right before the coronavirus pandemic began grounding flights over the Atlantic. We made a lot of videos together and became good friends. I found that YouTubers across the world have lots in common and plenty to discuss.

Tom and Juji eventually fell out, but Juji's channel lives on.

Close to Gorges du Verdon. On the hike there we met large dogs, that kept the wolves away from the feeding herd of sheep.

Free soloing, Les Gorges du Verdon, 2016. The route was 6b and easy, I felt secure and checked all the holds two times. I only free soloed the last part, the most spectacular.

*Selección Analogica, 9a+,
Santa Linya, 2016, the last
route of that difficulty I sent.*

Chapter 22

A Trip to Jordan

"Would you like to do a trip to Jordan?"

That question came in the fall of 2018 from photographer Jan Vincent Kleine. We'd been on several trips together and the tourism organization Visit Jordan was inviting us out to help attract more western visitors to the kingdom. I'd been to many countries, but not Jordan in the Middle East which has a population of just over ten million. It's not a country known for its climbing.

I had recently come back from a trip out to Tom and Juji where I lost my baggage. Then the same happened on a trip to Greece right before. So when I landed in Amman and my bag was nowhere to be seen on the carousel at the airport, I felt like I was on a losing streak. That was three bags in such a short space of time. "It'll come soon," I told myself, just as it did a few days later after the other two trips. All I had to do was check into my luxury hotel in Amman and wait. We were well looked after and everything was provided free of charge by our hosts.

All I had in my hand luggage was my camera and a few essentials. My checked bag contained all my climbing gear, a drone and other things for our month-long filming trip. I like traveling light, but there was a lot we needed on this trip. The drone was a particular worry as I'd heard rumors about a French YouTuber who was jailed in Jordan for using a drone. Apparently they were forbidden. Only rented drones with a military escort were permitted in this country with such tight controls over its airspace. Syria, Iraq and Saudi Arabia are all neighboring countries, so military activity is high.

There was a good group of us in Jordan, besides Jan Vincent and I. There was the legendary, 50-year-old German climber Alex Huber who was one of the biggest names in climbing at the height of his career. He was there with his dad Thomas, also a great climber. Huber Junior was still at the top of his game and swore on the old-school climber's diet, which involved plenty of beer in the evenings. Also joining us from the US was my ex-girlfriend Sasha Digiulian and a photographer. Our hosts arranged our itinerary and provided us with chauffeurs and local guides for our trip.

I liked Jordan. I liked the strange smells and the exotic sounds, the atmosphere in the Middle East, and I hoped that my baggage would arrive shortly, but it never did. I had to borrow climbing gear and other things when we headed north to a lush and vibrant part of the country.

One day we were out climbing in a newly established area in the north when we suddenly heard a loud rumbling sound. What was that? Thunder, somebody said. A tractor tire blowing out, said our hosts. But what about the fire that started up in the background? Me and the others were rattled.

Alex Huber said it couldn't be thunder. It had to be something else, possibly a missile. I put up a video expressing doubt about the noise, much to the disappointment of our hosts who didn't want any negative publicity. So in the next episode, I apologized for our concern and said it was nothing serious. Although that wasn't entirely true and we never did get a real explanation. I mean, we could feel the wall vibrate after the bang, and that doesn't happen when a tire blows out.

After a few weeks, Sasha and her photographer went home.

One day, Alex Huber and I went to do a route called *Jihad* on a 980-feet-high wall. On the way down Jan Vincent rappelled first, about 165 feet, while Alex and I stood at the top. We waited to hear that he was safely down at the next point but heard nothing. After a while we started calling down after him, but there was a lot of rock between us and we heard nothing back. Twenty minutes passed. He had to be safe on the wall, we thought. We loosened the fastener from the anchor while we held the rope and felt a certain tension in it – we looked at each other and realized that our buddy down there was not in safety, so we attached it quickly again, after about five seconds.

Jan Vincent had been down there shouting in vain, standing on a shelf and trying to get in against the wall. He was not an experienced climber and a situation like this was very frightening for him. Afterwards I said nothing about those sketchy five seconds, although I am sure I would have been able to hold his weight.

Wadi Rum, Jordan, 2018.
The route is easier than it looks.

Soon after, both Alex and his dad went home. That left just Jan Vincent and I as well as our local guide Washdi who drove our car, stopping occasionally in order to pray. There were reminders all around us that we were in a Muslim country. We saw few women or girls outdoors. A local explained to us that the reason women need to cover their faces is because they are like diamonds. One must not show off their diamonds but take good care of them and keep them hidden away, he said.

Washdi had expected to get more tip from Jan Vincent and went into a bad mood when he didn't. The mood turned ugly. The two of them began to bicker out there in the desert, at a camping site which had been our base for the last few weeks. Washdi drove an expensive Mercedes, which had been rented domestically but ordered by Mercedes in Germany for use as product placement in our videos.

Washdi had picked it up from the rental company and then crashed it, but he said nothing to Jan Vincent in the desert for fear of the consequences. An expensive car was serious business. Jan Vincent thought the car must have been already damaged when it was picked up and told Washdi's Jordanian boss. At night, Washdi snuck out in secret to try and fix the car. He also asked Jan Vincent and I to drive and took pictures as "evidence" that we had caused the damage.

He and Washdi really came to blows. The whole thing made my German buddy pretty paranoid and he asked me several times:

"Do you think that guy's crazy enough to kill?"

We slept in one tent and Washdi slept in the tent beside. The worry was that he was going to come in one night with a knife. I joked about sticking a post-it note with my name on it over my sleeping bag, so that I wouldn't be murdered by mistake.

But of course nothing at all sketchy happened and the days just slipped away from us as we spent our time climbing and getting to know the local big-shots who showed up. This one guy came along claiming to be a great climber, but he put his harness on back to front and didn't seem to have much of a clue. Another local hero who came to climb quickly gave up and disappeared with his tail between his legs. He never came back. The guys from the desert were brimming with confidence and they did own their turf, but the local climbing level in Jordan was pretty low.

Three days before going home, I got a message saying my luggage was finally at the airport. But I wasn't about to spend ten hours each way to go pick it up so close to the end. I'd have to just get it upon departure.

At the airport I asked: "Can't you just send the bag straight home again?"

"Nope, you have to collect it, go through security and then check it in again." This made me nervous. Four weeks in Jordan had made me paranoid. Was this all because of the drone? Did they know about the video on YouTube featuring the bang? Had they seen my videos?

I checked in the bag and one of the guards looked me right in the eye. They muttered something between them and seemed kind of secretive. But nothing happened. My baggage was swept away and I was free to go, much to my relief.

Overall, I had a great time in Jordan and I consider that trip to be one of the most special. It was not a pure climbing trip, but a varied adventure planned well by our domestic hosts.

Jihad 7b+, in the dessert of Wadi Rum, Jordan, 2018. Climbing gear borrowed from the locals. Alex Huber belaying. ▶

*Mammut sponsor trip, Cinque-Torri,
Italy, 2007. This was the first time I
saw a drone being used to film.*

Deep Water Soloing, Mallorca, 2016.

Chapter 23

The Art of Editing Yourself

YouTubers are not just like everybody else.

Well, for the most part. The difference is that the Magnus you see on YouTube is the edited version. Magnus edited by Magnus. The truth is, I worry that the viewers might be disappointed if they came face to face with the real me. In any case, I have no idea what impression people are left with after watching my videos, or whether it matches what they encounter when they meet me in real life.

On YouTube, I come across as a solid guy. The sort of person you can rely on, showing up with a new video almost every week. Somebody you feel like you know really well.

YouTubers are not movie stars, who are so rich and famous it seems as if they live on another planet from the rest of us. I'm not at all like that. I live in the same reality as everyone else and people often talk to me on the streets just like they would an old friend. Sometimes it seems like they expect me to recognize them even though we've never met before, and my distinctive Bergen accent tends to catch Norwegian people by surprise.

YouTube breaks down old barriers and creates a

closeness. I think this goes a long way to explaining why it feels natural for my viewers to come up and chat to me. Watching my videos is like being in a one-way conversation with me, and so it feels totally natural to continue it one-on-one.

"I like your videos" is a comment I get a lot.

Obviously it feels great to hear that, but I never know what to say back other than thanks. Each viewer has their own idea and impression of me which I can't know and won't always live up to. I probably seem different in real life to the Magnus on YouTube.

Most viewers can understand this if they think about it and put themselves in the same position. No person is just a freeze-frame or a magazine pin-up. It might seem that way when you watch somebody up on stage at a performance, at a show or in the movies. But not the rest of the waking day when they're just going about their business, constantly interacting with others.

Some people think that YouTubers are super extroverted because they expose themselves like they do. But that's not always the case. I consider myself an introvert and I like being alone. It's actually a necessary quality when you do editing by yourself. YouTube can mean a lot of time alone in front of the computer. That's also one of the main reasons why I like making videos, because I like figuring things out in my own head space. I think a lot of YouTubers are introverts who draw pretty much all the social contact they need from their videos and the responses they get.

An Idea

All of my videos on YouTube begin with an idea of a title and a thumbnail. It needs to outline the video but it can't be a con. Viewers shouldn't feel like they've been misled. The image needs to reflect the content behind it.

Viewers may spend as little as half a second choosing what video to watch, and often they'll go for bright and saturated looking videos, unconsciously. The most important information in the thumbnail should be to the left, because you read images the same way you read text. Getting clicks is what matters the most. Once they've clicked, they're in. Next you want them to watch as much as possible. YouTube's algorithms reward long viewing times and favor videos that people stick with. A good video is like a good wine; it gets better with time.

I often get ideas when I'm out hiking or running, and I write them down in the notes app on my phone right away. And then that's that. Movement gets your synapses firing and that's how good ideas are born.

The drawback of making a lot of videos is that you cycle through a lot of subjects. But the advantage is that new alternatives are constantly popping up, such as new activities and challenges. It means that my horizon can always suddenly expand.

Some ideas develop into a video while others don't, and I spend a lot of time studying watch time and how they interact. For example, I might scroll through a video and discover that a lot of people stop watching around minute seven. Then the question is to figure out why – perhaps because somebody's talking too much or there's not enough action?

I try not to joke around in my videos and I've never hammed up my sense of humor, even if my videos do make people smile occasionally. I'd describe my style more as playful, but not funny. Part of the reason is that it's very difficult to be funny in a second language. Sincerity is what matters most.

My videos often begin with a teaser. It's important that the pay-off doesn't come right at the start, but it shouldn't be buried at the very end either. Although it depends on the subject and the length of the video.

For me, YouTube is like a competitive sport: you need to bring your A game and do your best, put in the hard work and have plenty of endurance.

Viral is a term you hear a lot in the media. A video goes viral when it races around the world, often against expectation, and usually because its content is unique or surprising. For me in 2018, viral meant a video on YouTube reaching a couple of hundred thousand viewers. In 2021, the threshold is more like two million.

Posting Videos

Finishing a video is like turning in an assignment without knowing how many people it's going to reach. Videos that I've worked long and hard on have gotten few views, while snippets thrown together in a hurry have made a big splash. Although you can get some idea how well a video does, it's impossible to know exactly how many people watch it or to see their reactions.

Before I publish, my pulse increase. I check the title and description one last time. Then another time. I have already watched the video many times to be sure everything is as I planned. I know every second of the video. I always feel like it could be better, but eventually I have to publish it, even though I never get completely satisfied. The pace and rhythm in the video is the most important.

How the music blend with the pictures. The viewer is not supposed to notice the music, though it is some of the most important. Picking music takes a lot of time and has to fit the different parts of the video.

I normally post my videos between five and nine Norwegian time, when American viewers are awake as well. I watch the comments flood in, many per minute and right from the very first second. A full downpour of comments coming in from phones and computers all over the world. It's a huge kick. I think it's in our nature as humans to want to know what other people think of us, and I find it very rewarding to read so many positive comments after working so hard on something. Then there's also the likes and number of views – as a platform, YouTube gives you plenty of metrics to check.

I usually spend about an hour like this after posting a video, checking the comments and responding where it feels relevant. I always take some time to read the comments under each post, but then I put that video behind me to focus on the next. To move forward.

Being on the internet and on YouTube does something to your psyche. The thousands of positive comments I get awaken something inside and gives a really positive feeling. Confirmation of a job well done. It also motivates me to keep going and to make my videos even better. As a YouTuber, there's always something new to learn. The medium is evolving and nobody knows what corners it will turn or what YouTube will be like in ten or twenty years from now.

A Time-Consuming Job

Going out with the camera is like a treasure hunt for me. Capturing those special moments and images is like striking gold. It brings excitement and enthusiasm and the desire to transform what I've captured into a finished video. Then I go home with my memory cards filled with everything I've recorded and I transfer it to my Mac. No matter the time of day, even if it's three or four in the morning, I take the hour or so it takes to transfer everything on to my computer, to sort through and name all the files. Once that's done, I can fall asleep with a clear conscience and knowing that everything is in order, waiting to be edited.

I spend a lot of time on YouTube because I do most things myself, from the initial idea to the planning and editing. A twenty-minute video takes maybe two hours of recording which gets cut down to less than half and then trimmed down into the finished product.

I like doing everything myself and I think it's worthwhile. Some big stars on YouTube leave a lot or even everything to their team, but I think it's easy to lose authenticity that way. The videos become less personal. I want each video to feel like it comes directly from me. I get some assistance from Markus Skaane every now and then, but the rest is all me. In total, it takes around 30 hours to edit a twenty-minute video, plus recording time. Basically a whole working week, but I'll do seven days in a row if I need to and let each video take the time it takes.

"120 Boulders in One Session", is 53 minutes long and

took a whole 80 hours to edit. Videos like that are extra time and effort consuming, but all the more fun to perfect and to make as good as possible.

It's that same perfectionist spirit I have as a climber – for me, there is no middle ground. Either I give something my all or I don't bother. It's always been that way for me. Including in my relationships.

Marte

I was single between 2012 and 2019. Not having a girlfriend made sense at that time in my life, when I was traveling all the time and so focused on climbing.

There were a few girls here and there both in Norway and abroad, but they never developed into anything. Things went on like that for a while.

But in 2019, I started chatting with Marte from Ålesund on Instagram. I was on one of my travels to USA and the first month we messaged back and forth. The first thing I did every morning, and the last thing I did before falling to sleep at night, was to check if Marte was online and if she had sent me any new messages. I got a tingly feeling every time I saw a new notification coming in from Marte. The rushing sensation of butterflies in my stomach.

I thought to myself: "this isn't going to work, but let's give it a shot," and I had no expectations for how things would go.

She lived in the Bergen and I lived in Oslo, where eventually we agreed to meet, as she was going to Oslo to meet up with some friends.

But the chemistry was there and we quickly got together. We matched even better than I ever could have imagined. Marte is unlike any of the other women I've met. She's not just my partner but a close friend as well. We train together and like a lot of the same things, and have the same sense of humor. Plus, she's full of energy, which is great.

In Marte, I found a partner to share my life with, and we now live together in Oslo.

Miami, 2020, our last trip before the coronavirus.

Marte and I, home in Oslo, winter 2021.

Chapter 24

Changing Times

Climbing developed as a sport all through the 2000s. It became more of an elite sport, with its own brand of training and technique development, as well as new methods to improve performance. The level has gone up and its breadth has widened.

When I started, some of the older climbers in Norway thought what I was doing was advanced and professional, and that was probably true compared to their experience. But thinking back, I could have trained more efficiently. I experimented without knowing what worked best. It was trial and error. Today, there is so much more knowledge out there about what a climber should do to reach their optimal level.

In 2021, the sport is practiced in 75 countries and the number keeps going up by the year. The Japanese are getting really good at the moment and beginning to take the sport very seriously. It makes me wonder where the ceiling is, and how good the best can become. If somebody were to come along today with the talent of David Lama and the discipline of Adam Ondra, we might see a climber who can do a 10a route.

A lot has happened in climbing both in Norway and internationally since I first started back in 2000. The sport has grown and many now climb in their free-time, without being totally dedicated and often alongside other sports. Climbing has also become a commercial industry over the last two decades – a profitable economy has grown up around what was once an off-beat activity. Now there's a whole industry behind it, building walls, making gear and selling clothes. But even good climbers still don't make that much money.

Climbing became an Olympic sport for the first time in 2021. Better late than never, but if you ask me I think climbing should have been introduced to the Olympics much earlier. And I don't think the Olympics will turn climbers into well-paid super stars who get showered with attention and fame.

Many of the guys I competed against, like Adam Ondra and Jakob Schubert, are still active climbers today. Jakob won bronze at the Olympics in 2021.

Chapter 25

The Future

I never made a plan for my life. As a privileged guy from Norway, I've always counted on things working out and they always have. I've been lucky and had the chance to follow my dreams and meet a lot of great people along the way. Lots of opportunities and doors have been open for me.

Tuesday October 19, I reached 1 million subscribers on YouTube. It was special. When I started up, four-and-half years ago, I never dreamed of reaching out to this many people all across the globe. Some people have criticized me for being a YouTuber and promoting stuff other than what climbing is. But climbing means different things to different people. Some love being outdoors and value the experience of nature while others thrive best on an artificial wall and like being indoors. There is space for different varieties and no point in saying that one is better or more correct than another.

I have invested in Oslo Klatresenter and several other gyms and I have my own clothing brand, Rúngne, which is named after the strongest Jötunn in Norse Mythology. The

Jötunns were the opposites and the opponents of the gods.

We also build small unmanned climbing gyms through our ownership of the company Rúngne Buldr. Our ambition is to open these gyms across Norway and in other countries. The first one opened in Bergen in September 2021. If it goes well, we hope to become established across Europe from next year. The idea is to put small climbing gyms in places where this would have been unthinkable in the past, like smaller cities and towns.

My dream is to be truly financially independent and simply do what I want to – climb, travel and work with the things I enjoy. To live more or less like before. But perhaps it's more the idea of freedom that appeals the most. If my dream ever comes true, maybe I'll feel restless and want to go off and do something new. I like that feeling of moving forward and I like creating stuff.

It's cool that my videos are up there on YouTube, possibly forever.

And I don't like wasting time. Before all my time had to go into climbing. Now it's work and filming. YouTube and everything else. There's always something to be done and no two days are the same. Living without a routine suits me well.

I haven't got a degree in anything but I like to learn and I think it's fun to be involved in different projects together with others. So far, much of my work has revolved around climbing, but it would be cool to work with other stuff in the future.

One day I want to start a family and look forward to having kids and spending plenty of time with them. I hope to have a flexible job which will be like an extension of what I do now.

I've had an exciting life and I've been very privileged to work with what I love. Little did I know that all of this was going to happen when I first began climbing in Bergenshallen 21 years ago, just an innocent eleven-year-old-kid on the verge of finding his passion.

Afterword

On Wednesday May 26, 2021, I got a phone call asking me if I wanted to be a guest on a podcast about Australia. I said yes right away, but we kept on talking for a while. In part because the man on the other end of the line, Pål Skaugen, mentioned that his publishing house wanted to do a book about the climber Magnus Midtbø.

I had been following Magnus for a number of years. I had seen many of his videos on YouTube, and I was impressed by his physical capacity. I was curious to learn more about this guy who went about dangling off rock faces and hoisting himself up with one little finger. Who is this guy, I asked myself, and watched a few more videos without discovering all that much about his background – the actual story behind Magnus Midtbø.

That is what this book reveals. For the first time, Magnus tells how it all began, what motivates him to become the best that he possibly can within competitive climbing, about his training, his travels and his climbing life.

Thor Gotaas, Korsvoll, Oslo, September 2021

Bibliography Thor Gotaas

1999 *Tatere i norsk folketradisjon*

2000 *Taterne : Livskampen og eventyret*

2001 *På loffen*

2001 *«I motgang og medgang» : fotballen i Brumunddal gjennom et århundre*

2002 *Lirendreiere og lurendreiere*

2003 *Først i løypa : Historien om langrenn i Norge*

2004 *God skitur!*

2004 *Livslang skrivekløe*

2005 *Det Beste om Hallingdal i Nu*

2006 *Veldreidretten gjennom 100 år. Bind 1*

2007 *Skimakerne : Historien om norske ski*

2009 *Løping: En verdenshistorie*

2009 *Pihl – en sprek 175 – åring*

2009 *Skiløper og bureiser*

2009 *Det beste om Valdres i Nu*

2010 *Ørkenen Sur : den norske uteliggerkolonien i Brooklyn*

2010 *Først i løypa. Historien om langrenn i Norge.* Revidert og utvidet utgave

2011 *Skisportens vugge*

2011 *Fra bygd til by. Historien om Brumunddal*

2012 *Magnus «Wolf» Larsen. Sjømann og bokser*

2013 *Femmila. Skisportens manndomsprøve*

2014 *Th. Hansen : Familie Sagaen*

2014 *Fra bygd til by i bilder*

2014 *Alvdal : Historien om skiløperbygda*

2015 *Birken. Historien om det seige slitet*

2016 *Mitt liv som middels langrennsløper*

2016 *Josef Elvebakken. Eneboer og skogsarbeider i Nordre Land*

Informants

Jomar Bekkelien, Høyanger/Askøy, b. 1974
Hannah Midtbø, Bergen/Lommedalen, b. 1990
Magnus Midtbø, Bergen/Oslo, b. 1988
Tor Midtbø, Kristiansand/Bergen, b. 1961
Marius Morstad, Gran/Oslo, b. 1957
Merethe Rognan, Bodø/Bergen/Oslo, b. 1964
Knut Thorbjørnsen, Bergen, b. 1963
Kristoffer Kvamme Thorbjørnsen, Bergen, b. 1989
Henning Wang, Trondheim/Spain, b. 1984

Images